Restore Your Magnificence

A Life-Changing Guide to Reclaiming Your Self-Esteem

Complete Your Past
Assess Your Present
Design Your Future

by

Dr. Joe Rubino

Includes: The 12 Steps to Restoring Your Self-Esteem

Restore Your Magnificence:
A Life-Changing Guide to Reclaiming Your Self-Esteem
Dr. Joe Rubino

Vision Works Publishing
First Edition Copyright © 2003
By Dr. Joe Rubino

Published by Vision Works Publishing
(888) 821-3135 Fax: (630) 982-2134
VisionWorksBooks@Email.com

ISBN 0-9678529-9-4
Library of Congress Control Number: 2002104481

10 9 8 7 6 5 4 3 2 1

With This Book You Will:

- Uncover the source of your lack of self-esteem
- Complete the past and stop the downward spiral of self-sabotage
- Replace negative inner messages with new core beliefs that support your happiness and excellence
- Realize the secret to reclaiming your personal power
- See how you can be strong and authentic while using your vulnerability as a source of power
- Design a new self-image that supports your magnificence
- Create a vision for your future that honors your most important values
- Access the power of self-motivation and positive intention
- Accurately assess your strengths and weaknesses
- Design a specific action plan to live deliberately
- Realize the power of forgiveness
- Learn to suspend judgment and love yourself and others
- Discover the secret to un upset-free life
- Rid yourself of destructive anger
- Re-establish your worth and reinvent yourself to be your best
- Set and accomplish goals en route to designing a life of choice
- Create a vision of a life of no regrets
- Use visualization and affirmations to support your new self-image
- Champion others to maximize their self-esteem
- Learn to raise children and champion others to maximize their self-esteem

At an early age, we all decide that we are somehow unlovable, not good enough and not worthy of the best life has to offer. By discovering the source of our lacking self-image, we can re-interpret our past, reclaim our self-esteem and design our future deliberately and with power.

— Dr. Joe Rubino

Praise for "Restore Your Magnificence"

"I enthusiastically recommend *Restore Your Magnificence* to everyone interested in elevating his or her self-esteem. I have personally seen with tens of thousands of people how low self-esteem can underpin everything from health and wealth to relationship issues. *Restore Your Magnificence* is an opportunity given to all — seize the opportunity and take this book home today!"

– Eldon Taylor, PhD
Author, *Soaring Self-Esteem*
Inner Talk® subliminal technology

"*Restore Your Magnificence* is a brilliant roadmap to happiness, accomplishment, and to becoming an unstoppable person. Apply the principles and you will experience a newfound sense of worth and inner peace."

– Cynthia Kersey
Author, *Unstoppable*

"*Restore Your Magnificence* is an inspirational guide to realizing a life filled with meaning, purpose, peace and joy. Empower your life with this book and witness the blessings that high self-esteem will bring to your world."

– Tiffany Windsor
CEO, Inspired Lifestyles

"I have personally used this program's principles to support thousands of people to be self-confident, happy and prosperous. You owe it to yourself to read this book."

– Dr. Tom Ventullo
President, The Center for
Personal Reinvention

"This book by Joe Rubino could be the most important piece of material a human ever studies, whether they take it on as a young adult or later in their years. Self-esteem is the root of all evil or abundance. We all can build it 'by design,' as opposed to taking what we made up for ourselves as a very naive two-year-old. Study this book for 'life'!"

– Richard Brooke
Author,
Mach II With Your Hair On Fire: The Art of Personal Vision and Self-Motivation

"Dr. Joe Rubino has taken a complex psychological dynamic, which renders many of us dysfunctional, and mapped out a common-sense, sure-fire path to overcoming our lost magnificence! This book is great!"

– Robert Hickey
Clinical Psychologist &
President, Kansas Foundation
for Behavioral Health Managed Care

Dedication

This book is dedicated to you, the reader, and to your inherent magnificence and the magnificence within all human beings, even though we may forget this. It is further dedicated to those who have courageously declared to the world who they are and claimed their power. Their example of risking and living boldly and with passion inspires us all to be our best.

Contents

Section One: Complete Your Past

Chapter

Section Two: ASSESS YOUR PRESENT

Chapter

Section Three: DESIGN YOUR FUTURE

Acknowledgement

I wish to thank and acknowledge my mentors, Mike Smith of The Freedom Foundation and Carol McCall of The World Institute Group, for their contributions to my own personal development and to many of the concepts in this book. The fundamental principles that their work conveys form the foundation upon which self-esteem is built and nurtured. Their belief in the magnificence of all human beings has inspired me to champion people to be their very best. The majority of principles presented in this book are directly derived from the work of Smith and McCall. They, in turn, learned these concepts from their mentors, who learned them from theirs. In fact, many of the principles can be traced to the work of philosophers such as Fernando Flores, Martin Heidegger, Plato, Socretes, Christ and others.

Special thanks also go to my lifelong friend and business partner, Dr. Tom Ventullo, whose brilliant, intuitive insights continually champion people to reclaim their self-worth and maximize their dignity and ability to contribute to others. Tom shares my commitment and vision to impact the lives of 20 million people through our company, The Center for Personal Reinvention, www.CenterForPersonalReinvention.com.

Thanks also to my wife, Janice, and to my family for their love, support and undying belief in me. Their encouragement makes my work possible.

Sincere appreciation also goes to Richard Brooke, CEO of High Performance People, for his contribution regarding the areas of vision and self-motivation.

I also acknowledge the thousands of friends, colleagues and visionary partners who have worked with us to contribute the gifts of self-empowerment to others.

My sincere gratitude and appreciation extends to the thousands of courageous friends who have attended our courses at The Center for Personal Reinvention, participated in coaching sessions and given of themselves in the work we do. By bravely sharing their humanity and vulnerability, they and others have grown in self-love and enhanced their ability to be a contribution to the world.

And, lastly, thanks to you, the reader, for your courage and commitment to read this book and take on the exercises given so that you might realize the gift of enhanced self-esteem for yourself and others. We are all magnificent. It's about time we realized it.

Section One:
Complete Your Past

Chapter 1

The Essence of Self-Esteem

Enhancing self-esteem is 80 percent about completing your past and 20 percent about designing your future.

Noted psychotherapist Nathaniel Branden, Ph.D. defines self-esteem as "the disposition to experience oneself as being competent to cope with the basic challenges of life and of being worthy of happiness." To live a life marked by competence, fulfillment, contentment and accomplishment, you need high self-esteem. Healthy self-esteem sets a foundation for developing respect and empathy for others. It gives us the basis for accepting responsibility for our actions and for gaining satisfaction from our achievements. Those possessing healthy self-esteem are more likely to both create dreams and pursue them intentionally. By believing in their ability to accomplish these ideas, people with high self-esteem motivate and challenge themselves to grow and risk as they fully experience life. They don't allow the inevitable challenges and criticisms to discourage them from pursuing their worthwhile goals. People with healthy esteem possess the ability to love themselves — a prerequisite to love and be loved by others. In every way, a healthy sense of self-worth is a necessary requirement to leading an empowered life marked by positive self-direction, trust, responsibility and accomplishment.

We often see low self-esteem associated with criminal activities, drug and alcohol addiction, poverty, violent behavior, eating disorders, educational dropouts and low socio-economic status. Those lacking self-esteem don't do themselves any favors, but often display aggressive, egotistical, harmful and defensive behavior along with a lack of empathy.

Healthy self-esteem goes far beyond only possessing a good physical self-image. Too many confuse self-esteem with vanity, arrogance or self-centeredness. In fact, such qualities typically indicate a lack of healthy self-esteem. Physically attractive people may also have self-esteem issues. Having authentic self-esteem means feeling good about how you see yourself, as a happy person of high intrinsic value and contribution, able to produce a worthwhile result in your life and others. People possessing this quality have confidence not only in themselves but also in their ability to influence others in a positive manner. They act decisively and show respect for others by taking responsibility for their actions rather than casting blame, avoiding risk and fearing failure.

As humans, we are all magnificent by nature. We possess the ability to overcome obstacles, achieve meaningful accomplishments, honor our most important values, attain happiness and contribute our special, unique gifts to others. In short, we can take responsibility for making our lives work optimally. Unfortunately, through the course of experiencing life's challenges, we often lose sight of these facts. From birth and continuing throughout our lifetimes, we encounter countless experiences that can either enhance our self-esteem or erode it. The process of diminishing our self-esteem begins with a simple observation that we somehow do not measure up. We judge ourselves as different and deficient in some way. We decide that we don't belong. From this point, our lives unfold in accordance with our expectations. These expectations directly relate to how we feel about ourselves. Either we are worthy of all the good things life can offer or we deserve pain and suffering because we lack value.

When we judge ourselves harshly, we dramatically diminish our ability to merit love and achieve the success and abundance the world reserves for those most valuable. When we base our actions upon the belief that we lack what it takes to deserve rich relationships, material wealth and happiness, we trigger those very things we fear most: As our self-esteem insidiously continues to diminish, we find ourselves incapable of directing our lives and fortunes productively. Resignation sets in like dry rot, killing our spirits. This ensures that deeming ourselves as undeserving will viciously cycle into results consistent with this expectation and reinforces our sense of worthlessness. The lower our self-esteem drops, the less likely we are to act in a way that will generate positive feedback to elevate our deteriorating self-worth.

For most human beings, for a certain time after birth, life is good. Our parents meet our every need while providing us with the love and security we come to depend upon to develop into self-assured, well-adjusted individuals. Early in life, we learn to attach a value to the identity we create for ourselves. In this book, we will explore in detail how something happens during this process of self-discovery, sometime between birth and adolescence, to have us begin the process of judging ourselves harshly. Whether an event occurs or someone makes a remark, somehow we decide that we do not measure up in some way. This psychological trauma or series of traumas can range in severity from an abusive experience to a simple misinterpretation. For some, it may involve sexual or physical abuse or the experience of being abandoned or terrorized. It may start with a simple spanking or be as extreme as a beating. Something happens that plants the idea that they are not worth loving. The event need not look severely traumatic to anyone else. To be damaging, it just needs to disturb the inner peace and identity of the person experiencing it.

In any event, the result is the same. We start to compare our essential self to others and to feel bad about who we are in that comparison. This negative self-opinion begins distorting our relationship to others. Seeing ourselves as inadequate, we now respond differently to daily situations. Our results match our distorted self-image. This reinforces our feelings of unworthiness by providing us with concrete evidence to justify them. In short, we have created a self-fulfilling prophecy. The label we affix to describe our condition further compounds our feeling of inadequacy. Our self-esteem suffers more. So before we know it, we have built into our lives as fact that we are not good enough and are surely unworthy of love, abundance and happiness.

This self-judgment brings with it enormous pain. Because our inherent human nature has us instinctively seek out pleasure and avoid pain, we alter our behavior in an effort to avoid further rejection. Barraging our internal conversations with constant criticisms and dire warnings, we protect ourselves from potentially painful relationships and avoid communication, interaction and risk. We give up on our dreams and lower our expectations for fear of being hurt. We settle for less and then justify our actions to protect us from further harm. Resignation and the slow, subtle death of our spirit, with the resulting loss of vitality, inevitably result from our worsening self-opinion.

Loss of self-esteem can pervasively infiltrate every aspect of life or it can be limited to particular situations or circumstances. The latter occurs when you determine that you are inadequate in some domains but not others. Perhaps, you might feel good about who you are in business matters but suffer a poor physical self-image, thinking you are unattractive. Maybe you realize you excel in sports, but you have little self-confidence socially. We all have our strengths and weaknesses, areas where we feel confident and others where we feel lacking what it takes to fit in and do well. This limited type of diminished self-esteem, relegated to one or a few specific arenas, can be much more easily managed and addressed. In contrast, the all-encompassing loss of self-esteem where we feel unworthy of happiness and not good enough to compare with others in most areas of life is much more devastating.

This pervasive loss of self-esteem can become a rapidly progressing self-fulfilling prophecy. We compare ourselves to others and find countless ways that we don't measure up. As we judge ourselves to be inferior, we blame ourselves for everything that goes wrong. We strive harder and harder for perfection, but can't shake the destructive feeling that everything we do is inadequate. We constantly amplify our weaknesses and label ourselves as stupid, ugly, a failure, hopeless and unlovable. Our smallest mistake or oversight gets magnified in our eyes to the point where we lose faith in our abilities to communicate, relate and perform effectively.

We fall into the trap of thinking that the entire world sees us as being as pathetic as we see ourselves. We then misinterpret people's generally harmless words and actions, thinking that they're pointing out how pitiable we really are. We consistently overreact to situations and statements because everything feels like a personal attack on our inadequacies.

Others then perceive us as strange and notice that our energy is off. Their reaction reinforces our fears. We damage our relationships and alienate ourselves further. This proves us right about how we saw ourselves in the first place and further erodes our ability to connect with others. The more the self-sabotage occurs, the less able we are to interact effectively.

Don't lose hope. We can reverse the downward spiral of progressively diminishing self-esteem. By identifying how we have lost confidence in ourselves, we can stop the erosion of our self-image. Doing so will allow us to focus on restoring the magnificence that is our true intrinsic nature. Restoring confidence in ourselves and in our ability to achieve happiness and fulfillment and tap into the world's abundance will soon follow. Let's start with a clear look at how we lose self-esteem, and then, more importantly, let's work to restore it and step into the magnificence that is our birthright.

The path to raising self-esteem is to recognize the painful past and leave it behind, to effectively manage negative self-talk and to deliberately design a future that is consistent with the person you have decided to be, a person you can be proud to know and love. We will expose the human mechanisms that kill our spirits as we provide a proven process for reclaiming personal power and passion for life. By providing you with the tools to reinvent who you perceive yourself to be, you will be empowered to impact others.

Suffering is always optional. By claiming responsibility for your life and magnificence, you will no longer be at the mercy of whatever obstacles cross your path. You will grow daily in the confidence that you possess the ability to impact others with newfound direction and purpose.

Challenge

Decide now to take on the personal development exercises outlined in this book. You have the ability to reinvent yourself, elevate your self-esteem and lead a fulfilling life. It all starts now with your decision to do so. Do not simply read this book from a passive perspective, like watching television. Instead, adopt an intention to apply the principles discussed and perform the exercises suggested with the knowledge that they will transform your life and restore your self-esteem.

Chapter 2
The Paradigm of Perfection

To the degree that you resist who you are, the condition you are avoiding will persist and your self-esteem will suffer. Fall in love with the person you are and manage your "stuff" moment by moment. Do this by managing your commitments.

A paradigm is a hidden assumption that is generally held by the vast majority of the population. Like air to the bird or water to the fish, a paradigm is typically invisible to those who hold it. It usually can't be readily analyzed or distinguished. It is simply an assumption that everyone makes that is understood to be valid. It pervades a culture and invisibly influences how people think and act.

For example, during the days of Christopher Columbus, a common paradigm was that the Earth was flat. Sailors knew better than to venture too far out to sea for fear of falling off the edge. Until Columbus came along and challenged the paradigm, it was just generally accepted that we live on a flat Earth. Few questioned this "fact" until Columbus's voyage to the new world proved it faulty. It was only then that a new paradigm about the Earth's shape was established, namely that the Earth is round.

During the early days of colonial America, the Puritans believed that there were witches. Everyone knew this "fact." They also knew that the way you dealt with witches was to burn them at the stake. This was an accepted practice and common knowledge.

Paradigms clearly shape the beliefs of the society that holds them. Each paradigm keeps us from seeing another paradigm. In our Western culture, there exists the paradigm of perfection. During our growth and development, each of us becomes intrinsically aware of what a "perfect" person looks and acts like, how he or she thinks and behaves. We learn early on what is acceptable and what is different and doesn't measure up. Although physical beauty is only one aspect of perfection, many of those lacking in healthy self-esteem start the process of self-destruction by judging themselves as unattractive, too short or tall, too fat or thin or somehow otherwise not measuring up to the physical or social standards set by our culture. The misconception that perfection is achievable is a setup for disappointment.

In our Western civilization, the perfect man is well represented by our most popular TV and movie personalities. Those we hold in the highest esteem are handsome, intelligent, strong and tall, drive luxury cars, are cultured and exude charisma. They are educated, in control of their emotions, and wield power. They are self-confident, rarely at a loss for words and decisive in their actions. We all know how the good guy in a movie should look and act, just as we know how the bad guy doesn't measure up to these same standards.

This paradigm of male perfection excludes. It says that if you are not white, handsome, tall, charismatic, and lack the qualities associated with a leading man, there must be something wrong with you. You don't measure up and aren't good enough to be held in the highest esteem.

Similarly, young girls grow up with a clear image of what a perfect woman looks like. She must be beautiful, thin, sexy and intelligent with the charisma and talents to hold a place of high esteem in society. Music videos parade a succession of beautiful, fit and talented women before our eyes, further reinforcing the notion that being attractive, thin, successful and charismatic is the way to be. We grow up learning exactly what constitutes the ideal standard of how a boy or girl, man or woman should be.

Media and television set the backdrop from which comparisons are difficult to avoid. As we will discuss in later chapters, the original notion that we do not measure up comes from a decision that we make early in life about ourselves, about somehow not being good enough, not worthy of love or respect and deficient in comparison to our peers. So, although the concept of unworthiness may not have originally stemmed from TV and the movies, those images of perfection serve to reinforce the already present notion of our inferiority. They provide us with a sharp contrast to what we have observed in the mirror, leading to the obvious conclusion that perfection is achievable, but not for us. Again, physical image may be just one component of low self-esteem. This condition goes well beyond physical unattractiveness to the very core of our worthiness as a person, impacting our ability to reach our goals and honor our values.

Out of a desire to avoid future pain and compensate for our tarnished self-image, we often try to exert increasing control over our environment. Perfectionism grows from that desire to control others and avoid being dominated. This behavior heightens opposition to our perfectionist tendencies and further alienates us from others, reinforcing the idea that we do not belong, are unlovable and not worthy.

Another paradigm that greatly influences our opinion about a person's worth relates to what they do. We hold certain professions in much higher esteem than others. We glorify certain jobs, consider others respectable and simply look down upon many. We typically hold our top leaders in the highest esteem, at least until they fall off their pedestal. Major league athletes and movie celebrities are admired and almost worshiped. They command the highest salaries. We hold physicians, and particularly surgeons, as those workers most worthy of admiration. Other health professionals like dentists, optometrists, podiatrists, chiropractors and nurses take their place in the hierarchy of respected professions. Attorneys rate lower than these professions but higher than bookkeepers, travel agents and shopkeepers – they may be stereotyped as unscrupulous but, we assume, they make more money. Laborers are toward the bottom of the pecking order, with the less educated and least skilled deserving the lowest status. Lower still on the worthiness chain are the unemployed or those needing public assistance. At the very bottom rung are the homeless, alcoholics, drug addicts, criminals and convicts.

For many, the first blow to self-esteem comes with a realization that they don't fit the model of perfection. They may be fat or short, have big ears, live on the wrong side of the tracks, come from a broken home or possess any of the thousands of other qualities that make them less desirable, not good enough and unworthy of belonging and being loved.

Many allow their perceived lack of perfection to prevent them from achieving success, wealth and status. They resign themselves to a life of mediocrity when they realize that they do not rank high on the value list because of their skills, education, job and social status. They lack accomplishments and misinterpret this as lacking value as a person. They equate their economic and social status with their self-worth.

Although the perceived social status of one's job does not guarantee a commensurately high level of self-esteem, low self-esteem will often cause a person to not excel and to not achieve those positions that command respect. We are all familiar with athletes who turn to drugs or crime and entertainment celebrities who commit suicide. So, having achieved an occupation with status does not necessarily guarantee high self-esteem. Nevertheless, how we compare ourselves to others does influence self-image.

These views teach us to amplify our weaknesses while we become blind to our strengths. The lower our self-image drops, the less clearly we see ourselves. We fall into the trap of thinking that the rest of the world sees us in the same unflattering light that we see ourselves. As the cycle of self-sabotage continues, we bring about our greatest fears. Through our expectations and actions, we create the "proof" that reinforces our low opinion of our worth. Then we get to be right about it and sink into the darkness of self-pity. This scenario need not be so.

Chapter 3

The Origins of Self-Doubt

Misinterpretations damage your self-esteem and run your life. Freedom comes from reinterpreting your past with compassion for your humanity and that of others.

Some of us first realized we didn't measure up when we discovered we did not fit the paradigm of perfection. We discovered we were the wrong color, size, shape or appearance. Maybe we smelled or dressed funny. Perhaps, we weren't cool and didn't meet with the approval of our peers. Or maybe, our parents yelled at us, disciplined us or ignored us.

For many, the first awareness of not belonging likely came as a result of something that someone said or did that caused them to feel separate and different. They concluded from feeling that way that there must be something wrong with them and accepted that conclusion as a fact about who they really were. Yet that "fact" was not reality, but a decision built from emotional reasoning.

Could two children from similar backgrounds and environments develop far different levels of self-esteem? The answer lies in each child's interpretations concerning life's events. The particular situation that precipitated negative self-talk may have appeared harmless enough to other observers. But if it represented an initial shift in the way the child perceived himself, it may have been the beginning of diminished self-esteem.

This book will provide the tools to transform those early interpretations leading to a cycle of continuing erosion of self-esteem. You can learn to analyze negative self-talk and successfully shift to viewing yourself and others in a more positive light. Your ability to elevate your self-esteem will depend upon your willingness to implement the new skills you are about to learn and to create positive self-talk on a moment-by-moment basis for the rest of your life.

Exercise

In what ways do you consider yourself not good enough, less than perfect or not worthy of love and abundance? In addition to detailing your weaknesses, list your strengths. Decide now to further develop your strengths and seek excellence instead of perfection, realizing that perfection is unattainable.

Chapter 4

Transform Your Self-talk from Negative to Positive

Only you can diminish your self-esteem and only you can restore it. Freedom comes with non-attachment to whatever another says or does.

The key to reversing the process of self-doubt lies in creating empowering interpretations about what others say or do rather than interpretations that berate us and fuel feelings of inadequacy. Become skilled at distinguishing facts from interpretations.

We, too often, confuse what was actually said or done with the personal meaning we attribute to these occurrences. Those who suffer low self-esteem share a greater tendency to tack negative meanings onto life's events. The significance they place on these situations has negative personal connotations, even when none were intended or existed. These damaging interpretations immediately trigger anger, sadness or fear. These emotions rapidly become familiar and induce a false sense of security. Although we hate feeling angry, sad or afraid, we continually create explanations of events that land us in these moods.

Later in this book, we will explain how our human machinery takes full advantage of the power of these strong emotions to keep our low self-image in place. We continually collapse facts with interpretations. The stronger the emotions become, the greater our tendency to attribute incorrect connotations to situations. The more we do so, the further our self-esteem erodes.

The good news is that anyone can learn new behavior of attaching positive or neutral meaning to things that are said or done, replacing the typical negative implications. The first step requires developing the ability to distinguish facts from the interpretations we attribute to the facts. This is especially useful during times of stress and upset, when the emotions of anger, sadness or fear are present. Like red flags, these emotions warn us that we are confusing facts with interpretations, triggering the negative self-talk that eats away at our self-esteem.

Let's examine this destructive self-talk in detail. Picture your negative self-talk as a cynical character that clings to your shoulder that we'll call Chip. It's important to distinguish Chip's disparaging voice as an entity separate from and outside yourself. Chip can be male or female and will often take on the persona or qualities of a disapproving parent or early detractor. It is important to distinguish between Chip's pessimistic counsel and the wise guidance of your intuition and conscience. The former is skeptical and fear-based while the latter reflects wisdom and inner insights. Your intuition is never wrong. It is the knowing, inner light that guides you through life's turbulent seas.

In contrast, Chip may be single-minded but not very valuable in championing your excellence or making you feel good about yourself. His job is to either keep you unimportant and

Meet Chip! Clearly picture your negative self-talker as a character who exists to put you down, ruin your relationships and keep you small.

protected from risk or on the treadmill forever trying to do better and become worthy. He does this best by whispering nonsense into your ear that causes you to feel bad about who you are. This results in two common scenarios. The first has you sell out your needs and dreams, avoid new situations and shrink away from your true magnificence. The second has you driven to achieve and prove Chip wrong about how unworthy you are. Maybe you recognize having played out both scenarios in different parts of your life.

Let's examine the first situation. Chip likes when you become a victim as this makes his job easier. Victims don't belong. People don't like them and they don't look good. Victims also don't risk outside their comfort zones or aspire to any great (and dangerous) accomplishments. They live in a world marked by resignation, a world that excludes them as not good enough to play.

Chip can have you mistakenly believe that it is safer to hide out, quit trying and give up than it is to reach for the stars or go for the gold. He'll have you believing that it's actually better to play it safe, avoid risk and circumvent failure. He is quick to point out all the reasons why you should feel bad about who you are. He prefers that you believe his put-downs so that you will not think yourself worthy enough to try new ventures and find success or freedom. If you don't try, you can't fail, and so Chip will have protected you from that unpleasant possibility. He knows that by listening to his guidance, you will mangle your relationships and sabotage your success. He considers both unnecessarily risky and, like an overprotective master, prefers you to stay home and hide under the bed rather than lead the hunt. He'd rather you get angry at yourself for being a loser than risk a worse fate by overstepping your abilities. Chip is also the master of guilt. By reminding you of all the times you messed up, were selfish, hurt others, and fell on your face, he causes you to beat yourself up repeatedly. By doing so, in a contrary way, you actually feel better knowing that you have been properly punished for your transgressions.

Chip may tell you that life is not so bad if lived quietly, without the stress that accompanies the need to accomplish great things. Maybe you rationalize that you are not experiencing all the bad extremes by playing life on a small scale and beneath your potential. But perhaps, your life is dimmed, void of the passion and power that would be possible to experience if you lived your life with enthusiasm and daring. Restoring a healthy sense of self-respect will support you to reclaim your magnificence and generate a variety of new possibilities for happiness and accomplishment.

Chip also can run your life by convincing you that you can overcome your unworthiness if only you try harder and strive for perfection. He has you convinced that your worthlessness can be managed or camouflaged if you climb to the top of that ladder that's leaning against the wall of flawlessness, with the end of the ladder obscured in the clouds above. Once you reach what you think is the top of the ladder though, you discover that you're still not perfect, haven't accomplished nearly enough to counter your worthlessness and must continue to climb the ladder until you reach that faultless state. Of course, the ladder never ends. Perfection always lies disappointingly out of reach and mistily out of sight, and you get to continually beat yourself up as you drive yourself to achieve an unreachable objective. The more Chip berates you as not being good enough, the harder you try to be worthy – which you equate with being perfect. Coming from this powerless state of self-flagellation, you are less likely to be your best and achieve to your potential. There is no peace in this setup.

In either scenario, Chip succeeds in shattering your self-esteem and messing with your ability to separate fact from your negative interpretations. Either way, you easily resign yourself to always being less than magnificent. Reclaiming your self-esteem will stem from recognizing when Chip is speaking his nonsense and realizing that his misguided counsel does not support your excellence, happiness or magnificence. Guilt is always optional. Give up fruitlessly berating yourself for your faults. Now you can learn to aim for excellence, not perfection, and to respond in a manner consistent with your vision, values, commitments and life purpose.

Many of the derogatory messages that Chip whispers did not start with us. We didn't always program the disparaging phrases or misinterpret words or actions that cause our self-esteem to suffer. Many times we were actually told that we were not good enough, unlovable or unworthy of the best things in life by others. However, we did accept and absorb someone else's belittling delusions. Perhaps, a parent, grandparent or other person told you that you were flawed in some way and you believed them. Chip now may take on this person's words to remind you of your inferiority. Whether your derogatory thoughts originated from your own misinterpretations or from the unkind words of others, you still have the ability to recognize that these thoughts are untrue and do not support your happiness. You possess the awesome power to stifle your critic every time he or she speaks those critical words.

Chip will never go away for as long as you live. He lives to create dissatisfaction regarding who you are at the core and what your life is about. The more upset, strife and suffering he helps create, the worse you feel about yourself and the more Chip is validated. You will find Chip to be especially vocal during times of stress or upset. He uses these opportunities to remind you of how poorly you measure up. The best you can do is to recognize his misguided intention to either protect you from harm or motivate you to be better – and then put in emotional earplugs so you can't hear his sabotaging messages. Recognize his voice when he speaks his belittling opinions and know that you need not listen to what he says. His imprudent, distrustful advice puts you down, ruins relationships and promotes upset. The most effective way to temporarily silence Chip is to forcefully tell him to SHUT UP and TAKE A HIKE! You need to be as forceful in silencing his cynical chatter as he is in continually dishing it out. Your ability to discern between Chip's dominant disparaging voice and the softer wise counsel of your inner intuition will support your self-esteem to prosper.

Exercise

Learn to expose and counteract Chip's mischief. For the next week, as you go about your day, notice each time Chip puts you down, makes you wrong and keeps you small. Discern and record each negative thought you have about yourself and immediately state a positive correction in writing. Clearly differentiate Chip's voice from the voice of your trusted intuition and challenge his false messages. Note how each cynical thought serves some negative purpose. Perhaps it makes you feel superior about something, allows you to dominate others or protects you from risk. Maybe it drives you to succeed, to berate yourself with guilt or pity or to avoid seizing responsibility for your magnificence. Half the battle in silencing Chip is to recognize when he is speaking to you and specifically reinforce the realization that his counsel is nonsense.

Chapter 5

Separate Facts From Interpretations

If your self-esteem is low, your focus is likely on yourself.

Of course, we all think we know the difference between facts and interpretations. But do we? Facts are actual happenings, void of opinions and insinuations. Facts are black and white. They are literal events that transpire and the exact words uttered in a particular situation. Exactly what someone says or does is a fact. A respected news journalist or crime-scene detective reports only the facts.

In contrast, our interpretations attribute *meanings* to what was said and done. We are so accustomed to confusing these manufactured meanings with what actually happened that often we can't distinguish between the two. This is especially true with regard to what others say and do. Two different people can witness the same scene or hear the same statement and reach two entirely different conclusions about what was said or done or meant. Each swears that his or her version is the truth. But what both forget is that when it comes to what people say and do, there is no absolute reality, only each person's perception.

We all view the world based upon our past experiences, beliefs, prejudices, needs and emotional states. No two people will experience an event exactly the same way. In fact, the same person may perceive a situation differently if he is tired, preoccupied, angry, ill or in an altered mental state. What we think is our objective reporting of an event is really the personally flavored version we create based upon the meaning we attribute to the facts, usually influenced by deep-seated assumptions and biases that we're not even aware of.

How we interpret another's words is also a function of the way we listen. Listening from a positive or negative, accepting or judgmental, angry or easy-going state will affect our interpretation of what we hear. Our listening attitude never lies empty like a blackboard that has yet to be written upon. Instead, all our beliefs, opinions, hopes and fears fill it up. We frequently do not hear exactly what people are saying or intending to imply. In fact, we can only hear something if we have a background from which to interpret what is being said. Some people have a generous listening style or attitude, giving others the benefit of the doubt. Others come with a critical listening style, as though waiting to find fault. To effectively change the way you listen, first identify how it is that you listen. Then decide to consciously shift out of that automatic habit into a new, purposeful, empowered listening attitude. See the chart on page 35 for some examples of both automatic and deliberate ways of listening. Identify your typical listening style and decide to listen in a new and empowering way. All it takes to listen differently is to recognize when you are listening in a way that doesn't support you and intentionally shift into listening with a receptive manner that does. For a more in-depth discussion of listening skills, please refer to my book *The Power to Succeed, Book II: More Principles for Powerful Living.*

By training ourselves to distinguish facts from interpretations, we can successfully avoid many of the misunderstandings that lead to daily upsets. All too often, we think we are speaking about facts when we are actually interpreting what is so.

For example, the statement, "Jim is a jerk," may seem like a fact to those who share this opinion, but it is really an

Common Automatic Listening Styles*

- I already know that
- Hurry up and get to the point
- Agree – Disagree, Right – Wrong
- Do they like me?
- To look good
- To be offended

Empowered Listening Styles*

- To learn something new
- For the value, regardless of style
- To consider non-judgmentally what is said
- To contribute to the other person
- To empower the greatness of others
- Without attachment to what is said
- For what it's like in the other person's world

**Adapted from the teachings of Mike Smith and Carol McCall*

interpretation about the things Jim does. Saying, "Jim yelled at his wife and son and kicked his dog" is a factual statement. It is what is so. No judgment is being rendered. In contrast, when we take what happened and provide an opinion about it (that Jim is a jerk), we unleash an emotional energy tied up with our judgment of what it means to be a jerk. From Jim's perspective, he acted in the way that people who are angry act. He learned this behavior by observing his own dad act in a similar manner. It is the only way he knows how to express his anger. Although, we may not approve of Jim's behavior, we can see how he may not share in the judgment that he is a jerk.

Similarly, if we witness a woman spanking her child, we might say, "the woman is abusive and cruel" and think we were reporting on what is so. But, perhaps, the woman grew up with the belief that mothers who love their children discipline them as a sign of their affection. Her actions may stem from her commitment to her child's excellence. So, you see, "abusive" or "cruel" are interpretations of the situation. The facts are simply that the woman spanked the child. To that woman, perhaps not spanking the child would, in her mind, reflect a lack of love and thus be cruel and abusive behavior.

The underlying biases for these misinterpretations often go back to our childhood. Thinking they were teaching us right from wrong, our parents frequently labeled us as "bad" when our behavior did not meet with their approval. We were bad if we spoke out of turn, cried, didn't finish our dinner, left our room messy or fought with our brothers and sisters. In an effort to control our behavior, our parents or guardians branded us with all sorts of labels like bad, lazy, slow, stupid, fresh, wild or selfish. By becoming angry with us and seeming to withdraw their love, they appeared to repeatedly chastise our very worth, not just our unacceptable behavior. We took these frequent angry moral thrashings to heart and retained the stigma and accompanying guilt long after the actual incident may have been forgotten.

With respect to interpretations that damage self-esteem, the concept of failure is a big offender. We accept as fact that failures are real and that they are bad. We mistakenly think that there are failures we experience and these reflect upon our value as a person. The notion of needing to avoid failure has us give up on our dreams and run from any situation where the prospect of failing looms. However, if we consider that there is no such thing and that failure exists only as an interpretation, we can develop some power regarding such situations.

Let's reconsider past situations labeled failures, instead, as valuable learning experiences. Such encounters are simply part of what it means to be human. When we no longer focus upon finding our own flaws, we cease to look at experiences as opportunities to invalidate our worth. We can look more powerfully at the valuable growth we gained from such instances. By accepting that these situations legitimately contribute to our growth, we can actively embrace "failure" as an active learning experience, create a ton of it and realize the benefits that come from exploring new territory.

It's important to remember that we all suffer from misinterpretations from time to time. However, for many with low self-esteem, this trap of misinterpreting what others say or do can be particularly damaging. A common habit of many with low self-image is to interpret the words and deeds of others as though they were intended as a personal affront. While not all people with low self-esteem share this trait, those displaying this tendency have others needing to walk on eggshells when around them. The more distorted the person's sense of reality, the more certain they will be that their impressions are accurate and that the world is out to get them. If left unchecked, this distortion can rapidly progress to a state of paranoia.

If you tend to become easily offended, commit instead to unendingly recognize this tendency to harshly judge what others say or do and rigorously choose to interpret life in a way that carries no offense. This supports your happiness and results in effective,upset-free relationships. As your self-esteem improves, this skill will improve. The need to manage these potentially offensive misinterpretations will always exist. The challenge is never over and the danger remains to fall back into upset as soon as this is forgotten.

Dealing effectively with people who regularly experience severely distorted interpretations of reality will require empathy. Realize their responses align with the view of the world they are experiencing. They are doing the best they know how in line with their misguided sensory input. Lovingly support them to continually reinterpret what others say or do in a way that carries no personal offense. This will assist them in realizing a newfound peace.

Exercise

1. Identify your most common automatic listening styles. How do these negatively affect your self-esteem? What new empowered listening styles will you generate to support your relationships and happiness and boost your self-image?

2. Reflect upon a recent upset you experienced. Rigorously distinguish between the facts of exactly what was said or what happened from the meanings you manufactured about the facts. How do your misinterpretations diminish your self-esteem?

Chapter 6

Moods

We will sacrifice our health, relationships, love, peace, possibilities and happiness just to be right. Give up your right to be right, and your self-esteem will flourish.

Like glue, our moods bond the misinterpretation mechanism in place. We observe a factual situation. We immediately apply some meaning to what was said or done. This interpretation sends us into our most familiar mood. For the most part, this mood gets triggered as anger. The anger is typically first directed at those we blame for treating us unfairly, but it can also be directed inwardly at us, devastating our self-worth. The anger also will have a flavor to it that is influenced by the judgment we make. It might be indignant anger (How dare you!) if we judge that we or someone else has been unjustly wronged. Perhaps the anger may be marked by righteousness (I can't believe you could do something so...). It might span the gamut from irritated or disgusted anger to full-blown rage, depending upon how dramatically the episode triggers our sense of right and wrong.

This angry mood often comes with a physical response. Some people become hot or red in the face. Others feel a tension or pain in their jaws as they clench their teeth or may feel the hairs rise up on the back of their necks. Some may be stricken with pain in their head or stomach. Become aware of your own physical reaction to any situation that triggers an angry response. This physical cue warns you that it is time to stop, drop and feel: Stop the action and take a minute to analyze exactly what is going on. Drop the negative energy and release the anger that has you react negatively toward the person triggering your mood. Feel the opportunity to reinterpret the situation and exit the destructive cycle that would lead to further erosion of relationships and loss of self-esteem.

For most, the mood of anger is the predominant emotion. Some rapidly transform the anger into sadness or fear. This can be such a familiar and speedy transition that these people will be primarily aware only of being sad or fearful, rather than angry. Often, this is due to their ability to immediately suppress anger, locating themselves in the more acceptable emotions of sadness or fear. People who have a tendency toward sadness will unconsciously scan for interpretations that will "make them" sad. If you tend toward a mood of sadness, recognize how often you take what someone says or does and interpret it so as to land you in your sad mood. The same applies to fear. If being afraid is your prevalent mood, you will use every opportunity to become frightened. You will interpret situations to be dangerous or scary while the same event would not trigger fear for those with a different mood.

Learning to reevaluate what others say without attaching a mood breaks the cycle that sabotages your magnificence, happiness and self-esteem. View the facts, not the interpretations, and escape the automatic moods that have trapped you.

Exercise

Reflect upon a few recent upsets. Identify your most prevalent mood. It will be some form of anger, fear or sadness. In each instance, distinguish the facts of what was said or done from any interpretations you created that generated your mood. Create a new and empowering interpretation about what was said or done in each instance that will result in your being mood-free.

Chapter 7

The Vicious Cycle

If you are a human being, you are a jerk – pretending you're not. Enlightenment is finding out that you are a jerk and that everyone else is as well. We cannot be magnificent if we do not allow ourselves the room to be jerks.

— Mike Smith
President, The Freedom Foundation

So, let's recap the problem. Someone says or does something. These are the simple facts that occurred. Buying into the premise that life is a difficult and dangerous struggle, you attribute some negative meaning about what they said or did. This interpretation makes you angry, sad or afraid or gives you some version of at least one of these moods. Everyone on the planet does this to some extent. It makes you right and separates you from others who you see to be as wrong or different.

If your self-esteem is not what it could be, start to notice how you attach negative connotations to words or events, causing you to feel poorly about yourself. Maybe you believe that the criticisms of others must be true. Perhaps you decide (or agree with others) that you are not worthy, do not belong, that no one likes you, that you are unattractive or stupid. Or you fabricate any number of other interpretations that do not allow you to be happy, effective or powerful in your relationships. It's time for you to realize that you need not buy into this negative self-talk or listen to the disempowering opinions of others.

Yes, it certainly looks like it is true. You are so accustomed to telling yourself or being told that you are less than others in some significant ways that you have come to believe that it must be so. It began early in life when you first accepted as fact that you didn't belong, were unlovable or did not measure up. You then looked out upon the world from darkened glasses that reflected this perspective. With this misguided outlook, you interpreted future events to reinforce your low opinion about yourself. The more you believed there was something wrong with you, the more your interpretations developed and built on this delusion.

The stronger the delusion became, the more your actions reflected a loss of self-esteem. Perhaps you isolated yourself socially. Maybe you became angry or violent or you resorted to aggressive or anti-social behavior. Perhaps you became arrogant in an effort to conceal your insecurity by intimidating others. Or, you might have become a meek doormat or people-pleaser in an effort to fit in and be liked. Maybe you turned to food, alcohol, sex or drugs in an effort to disconnect from the pain.

Whatever behavior you adopted, you did so to protect yourself and survive in what you saw as a dangerous world. You did the best you knew how in dealing with the way you perceived others. The good news is that you can now train yourself to see the world from a different, more positive perspective. This view will support you in acting differently. These new actions, in turn, will productively transform your relationships. People will respond more favorably toward you, and this positive reinforcement will support your self-esteem. So, let's examine exactly how to create these new and empowering interpretations.

Chapter 8

Manage Your Moods to Enhance Self-Esteem

Ninety-nine percent of people's reactions have nothing to do with you. One percent of what people are reacting to comes from the fact that your human-ness triggers something in them.

Ninety-nine percent of your reactions have nothing to do with them. One percent of your reactions are based in their human-ness triggering something in you.

— Carol McCall,
Author, *Listen, There's a World Waiting to Be Heard*

We want to disengage the self-defeating interpretation machine that we all tend to use. The key is to recognize when someone says or does something that activates your mood. Your mood of anger, sadness or fear (or some variation of these emotions) warns you to sit up and pay attention.

When you recognize these emotions striking, ask yourself the following questions:

1. What happened? Sticking to the facts, what was said or done?
2. What meaning have I given to what was said or done, causing me to feel angry, sad or afraid?
3. If I put myself in the other person's world and gave them the benefit of the doubt, what empathetic, mood-free explanation could I come up with to explain their actions?
4. Do I realize that their actions are not personal, even though they might appear to be on the surface? What was said or done is about the other person, not me.
5. How does this new, empowering interpretation contribute to my happiness and growing sense of self-esteem?

When we put ourselves into the other person's shoes and ask, "What must his or her world be like and what could they have been thinking for them to have spoken or acted as they did?" we take responsibility for realizing that no one can affect our self-image negatively except ourselves. As Carol McCall, expert on the art of listening, points out, 99 percent of an upset is about the person who's upset and only 1 percent is about the person who supposedly caused the upset. By creating new interpretations that allow for empathy, compassion and an appreciation for the other person, we alter our perception of the circumstances that occurred. We then feel better about the other guy, and our relationship strengthens. We move from a world based upon the past to a life in the present where we can deliberately design the future. We create our world anew instead of being at the mercy of past events that happened to us. This eliminates stress, which is always the result of faulty interpretations. By giving up our right to be invalidated, we nurture our magnificence and nourish our self-esteem.

The Old Pattern

Someone says or does something

You buy into negative opinions or create interpretations about what was said or done that disempower you, hurt your relationships and make you angry, sad or scared

You react to the mistaken images you've created in your mind about yourself and other people

Your behavior reinforces a drama cycle that continues to erode your self-esteem

You continue to misinterpret what others say and do or believe derogatory opinions, thus strengthening the cycle and diminishing your self-esteem

The New Pattern

Someone says or does something

You feel yourself landing in your mood as you become angry, sad or afraid

You recognize that your initial reaction was to believe the negative opinions or create negative interpretations that gave you your mood

You release the anger (or fear or sadness)

You reinterpret what happened so that your new interpretation keeps you mood-free and contributes to your self-esteem

You recreate your future, rebuild your relationships and thus reclaim your self-esteem

You ready yourself to interpret your next experience in an empowering way

Exercise

Reflect upon the last time you recall feeling upset. Answer the six questions presented in this chapter to create a new, empowering and mood-free interpretation. How does doing so support your self-esteem?

Chapter 9

Why We Keep Our Moods in Place

I told you I was sick!

— Headstone inscription (making its owner right)

You may say that you hate living in continual turmoil and are tired of being at odds with others and feeling bad about yourself. You may think this should be incentive enough to reinvent yourself and your interpretations. If the process of ***recognizing*** your mood, ***releasing*** the emotion, ***reinterpreting*** what happened, ***recreating*** your future and ***reclaiming*** your self-esteem is so simple, then why do we keep the old patterns in place?

The answer lies in the addictive nature of our moods! We hate being angry, sad and scared. But, like a heroin addict who hates being hooked on drugs but can't seem to pull that needle from his arm, so it is with our moods. Our moods keep us churning in the drama cycle of life. Though we dislike them, they are familiar and comfortable like an old habit. They make us feel alive.

Our moods provide us with several contrary pleasures and ironic benefits. They make us right and make others wrong. They allow us to feel we are dominating others or help us avoid being dominated ourselves. They make us a victim of our circumstances. As a victim, we get to feel sorry for ourselves. Victims attract the pity and sympathy of others. It is often easier to wallow in pity rather than take responsibility for making our lives work optimally. As we continue to suffer, our self-esteem dwindles further. Our lives seem full of things we don't want. We want all the things we don't have. We point to our low self-esteem in an effort to justify why life is the way it is. It's no wonder that we continue to suffer and feel bad about who we are! The more we hate having low self-esteem, the more we use it to justify why we can't reinvent our lives to be fulfilling and productive. Having low self-esteem gets us off the hook for turning our lives around.

Keeping our addictive moods and low self-opinion in place also has other ironic benefits. By reinforcing the feeling that no matter how hard we try, we still fail to measure up, we keep the game in place. We tell ourselves we will do better. That might mean trying harder, studying more or spending more time with the person we just can't seem to satisfy. Our life becomes dedicated to climbing over that next hill ahead that challenges us. We tell ourselves that if we can just crest this one hill, we will be worthy of praise and acceptance. So we do whatever it takes to make it up the hill. However, upon reaching the top, we find yet another, more important hill before us. We beat ourselves up for not having climbed high enough but recommit to taking on this new challenge under the assumption that arriving at the top of this next peak will make us good enough. Of course, the hills continue to appear, offering a constant series of new challenges to conquer. In an ironic way, the never-good-enough setup that drives us does produce some transient victories. These short-lived accomplishments allow us to take fleeting pride in what we have achieved. They also may be worthwhile feats, but we are too blind to accept that, too driven by the belief that who we are can never be good enough.

So, this structure permits us to retain hope in our ability to somehow overcome our unworthiness by achieving perfection and becoming whatever it is we fear we are not. It also protects us from lack by being forever driven to produce. However, before long, we revert back to the feeling that our latest achievement is hardly enough. We find ourselves back on the treadmill racing up the next hill, feeling bad about ourselves again. But continuing to take pleasure in self-pity — without taking responsibility for reclaiming our self-esteem — has profound costs. Identifying these costs can be the first step in generating the motivation to have this unwanted condition disappear.

Exercise

What are some of the major reasons for keeping your mood in place? What contrary benefits do you get from your addictive moods?

Chapter 10

The Costs of Not Reclaiming Our Self-Esteem

Suffering is having something you don't want or wanting something you don't have. Responsibility is the key to eliminating suffering and elevating self-esteem.

— Mike Smith
President, The Freedom Foundation

There are many costs associated with our reluctance to claim responsibility for empowering interpretations that source our esteem and excellence. One is in the arena of our relationships. We can develop richly rewarding relationships with others only if we hold ourselves as worthy of such contribution. Our moods and misinterpretations destroy the likelihood of workable relationships. They distance us from others and isolate us. We mistakenly assume that others see the same devastating faults in us that we see in ourselves. We expect them to reject us as unworthy of their friendship, love and attention. We become easily angered, sad or afraid. We avoid new challenges that might expose our faults. We isolate ourselves and shun social situations in an effort to protect ourselves from hurt.

Our actions anticipate rejection and actually bring it about as a self-fulfilling prophecy. We dismiss any of our own perspectives as wrong, sacrificing them for someone else's who must be more worthy because they're not us. We consistently shut down our own interests and viewpoints as being automatically flawed or worthless. When people appear to be interested in our friendship, we fail to set healthy limits or avoid responsibility for making reasonable requests for fear of being rejected. Or, taking another approach, we expose their flaws and reject them as unworthy of our friendship. After all, who would want to be friends with someone who would want us as their friend! We then cite these damaged relationships as evidence there is something terribly wrong with us, and so our self-esteem dwindles.

We pay another cost of low self-esteem with deteriorating physical and mental health. All physical and mental disease is the manifestation of an emotional condition. Sooner or later, low self-esteem and the resulting lack of emotional health will translate into a breakdown of the body. This is most obvious with heart disease and cancer. Withholding love for ourselves ages us prematurely. Our cells age and die and our bodies respond negatively from the deprivation of joy and happiness. We put on excess weight, develop ulcers and suffer sickness and disease. Or, in an effort to numb our pain, we attempt to escape into the oblivion of drugs, alcohol, isolation or other addictions. For a more thorough analysis of this concept, I suggest reading *You Can Heal Your Life* by Louise L. Hay. Hay explains how failure to love oneself is at the root of nearly all physical problems.

When you don't love yourself, you don't treat yourself with respect. You live along the automatic assumption that you're not worth taking care of – you neglect eating right, exercising, getting medical attention or looking after your well-being. Disease results from what's going on at a cellular level, fueled by a deprivation of love.

Loss of happiness, self-expression and vitality also stem from low self-esteem. Those lacking self-belief give up their ability to make a difference in others' lives. These costs spread to family members and afflict those closest to those lacking esteem. With the loss of happiness and self-expression comes loss of love, intimacy, partnership and affinity. It is difficult to love someone who does not love himself. Intimacy is a function of clean and open communication. Such communication is often the first casualty when self-esteem suffers.

Perhaps the greatest cost of not taking total responsibility for managing our interpretations is in the lost possibilities for our lives to be lived richly and with purpose. When our self-esteem suffers, we lose our potential for identifying and fulfilling our life's purpose. To take our focus off our own needs, faults, challenges and concerns, we must first believe in our ability to contribute to others. Contributing ourselves – not sacrificing, but freely giving renewable value — stems from both a commitment to serve and the knowledge that we have something worthwhile to offer. When we hold ourselves in low esteem, we short-change others as well as devaluing ourselves. We lose sight of our magnificence and forget that we all have special qualities, talents and gifts that would benefit others. Not taking responsibility for our greatness cheats the world as we sell out our potential to impact others with the special gifts that only we can offer. One way to handle this preoccupation with our fears is to focus on worthwhile achievements that are much more significant than our petty concerns. By committing to some worthwhile and lofty undertaking, we can get unstuck, take our focus off of our own concerns and problems and build our self-image in the process.

You can alter your destructive attitudes by pursuing the personal development principles presented in this book. But the vast majority suffering from low self-esteem, are blind to this conscious option. Awareness must come first. Rather than take on the challenge of reinterpreting life's events, most adopt various ways of protecting themselves in what they perceive to be a dangerous world. They resign themselves to do the best they can, knowing it will never be good enough. Let's look at what some of these survival formulas are.

Exercise

What are the costs of not reclaiming your self-esteem? Consider the areas of your health, relationships, vitality, happiness and ability to contribute to others. What prices have you already paid?

Chapter 11

Survival Formulas

Some refuse to develop their self-esteem, even after becoming aware of their ability to successfully do so. Having low self-esteem makes a person a victim. Victims feel sorry for themselves instead of accepting accountability for their excellence and for making life work.

Faced with the idea they are somehow less worthy or completely worthless, those lacking self-esteem protect themselves the best they know how. They see this being necessary in a world where they do not fully belong and are unlikely to thrive. In the interest of self-preservation, the human machinery adapts to outside situations in a myriad of ways. The goal is survival.

Some adapt by hiding out. Others take the offensive. Some become clever and outsmart the competition. Many become passive and look for others to take pity on them. Everyone has their own unique survival formula adopted at an early age to protect them from the apparent threat others represent. Since this protective behavior seemed to work at some time to keep them safe, they repeated or amended it as they grew into adulthood.

Some decided physical strength was the best means of protection, so they developed their muscles and learned the skills warriors possess in an effort to be stronger than their enemies. Others saw force as a means of exerting power. These people became the world's bullies, dictators and tyrants. Or maybe, they decided to dominate in a legal, acceptable manner by becoming policemen, soldiers or others in uniform. Possibly, they sought a title to gain the prestige they would need to control others or avoid being dominated. Still others decided the secret to survival was money and possessions. They developed a strategy to be richer and thus safer and better able to manipulate others. Others saw they could control best by honing their abilities. They became educated, learned special skills and sought to outsmart or outperform their adversaries.

In the end, survival strategies are all about gaining power to erase their feeling of being small and powerless. They share the assumption that what power we have inside us as a person is not sufficient to succeed or thrive in the world. We need to find a better way to compete and win out over others.

The next several case studies will elucidate how people respond to the dangers of living and how they endeavor to keep safe from these perils. All survival formulas are based on doing, not being. Because they view themselves as being dramatically flawed, they feel compelled to do something to externally deal with their defective nature. As such, the formulas are flawed and do not address the source of low self-esteem.

Happiness and a sense of self-worth must reside within us. They are not places to get to but a place from which to come. When we live with the confidence of knowing who we are and what our gifts are, we manifest our life-purpose. Our actions will then be productive and characterized by high self-esteem.

Case Studies

Not trusting is usually about us, not the person we mistrust.
Learn to trust others by trusting yourself first.
With elevated self-esteem comes increased trust.

All human beings lie at times. Courageously decide to trust and recognize that everyone makes mistakes.

Case Study #1

FACTS: Laura went to the eye doctor when she was 7 years old. The eye doctor asked Laura's mom to wait in the reception room while he examined Laura. The doctor sexually molested Laura and made her promise not tell anyone or else he'd hurt her family.

LAURA'S INTERPRETATION ABOUT HERSELF: She was bad to have tempted the doctor who complimented her on her pretty dress. She was a bad, dirty girl.

LAURA'S INTERPRETATION ABOUT PEOPLE: People will always hurt her and can't be trusted.

LAURA'S MOOD: Rage leading to fear.

LAURA'S SURVIVAL FORMULA: To hide and cheat in order to survive.

Laura accepted the blame for what happened in the doctor's office. She decided she was bad and it was her fault the doctor did what he did. Based upon this interpretation, Laura decided people can't be trusted and she couldn't trust herself. Laura decided that, in order to survive in a world where others lie, hurt and threaten little girls, she would have to be cleverer than they were and get what she could before they hurt her. Laura lied and cheated at every opportunity, becoming a habitual liar and con artist. She maintained a low profile in her personal life, avoided social occasions and had few friends. Her self-esteem suffered, and she assumed that she didn't belong. She also told herself that men couldn't be trusted and were interested only in sex. She married and divorced three times. Each time she trusted men less and considered herself a loser that no one really wanted to be with.

Case Study #2

FACTS: When John was 3 years old, his mom and dad brought home a new baby brother from the hospital. They told him they still loved him just as much, but they paid a lot of attention to the new baby.

JOHN'S INTERPRETATION ABOUT HIMSELF: He was not good enough because his parents needed another baby to replace him.

JOHN'S INTERPRETATION ABOUT PEOPLE: People lie and steal from you, just like his parents lied about loving him and his baby brother stole their love.

JOHN'S MOOD: Indignant anger (How dare you!)

JOHN'S SURVIVAL FORMULA: To be a people-pleaser and do whatever it takes to have people like him.

When John was 3 years old, he decided he was not enough for his parents. This explained why his parents would bring home a little intruder, his brother Jim. John decided that if he was to be allowed to stay around, he had better get his parents (and later others) to like him. His survival depended upon it! John became the teacher's pet in school and the dutiful son at home. He settled for jobs that paid poorly and never asked for a raise or time off. He was just happy to have any job at all. John went through life settling for less, with the motto "Don't rock the boat."

Case Study #3

FACTS: Linda's dad drank almost every day upon coming home from work. About once a week, he would get drunk and become violent, throwing and smashing things and hitting Linda and her brother, Michael. When she was 9 years old. Linda's dad pushed her out of his way. She fell down the cellar steps and broke her arm.

LINDA'S INTERPRETATION ABOUT HERSELF: She was bad and unlovable. Her dad didn't love her.

LINDA'S INTERPRETATION ABOUT PEOPLE: People don't care and are selfish.

LINDA'S SURVIVAL FORMULA: Don't let anything bother you. Don't feel emotions. Care even less than others do.

Linda felt rage at her father for hurting her. She then felt guilty for hating him when she knew she should love him. Linda decided at 9 years old that it was too painful to love anyone. All people did was hurt you, so it's safer not to care. She suppressed her emotions and refused to allow others to get close to her. She usually avoided dating and when she did, she would not let any relationship get serious. Her lack of close friends and intimate relationships proved to her that she was not worth loving.

Case Study #4

FACTS: Bill's dad died in a car accident when he was 5 years old, leaving him behind along with his mom and older sister. His mom said to him, "Bill, you're now the man of the family."

BILL'S INTERPRETATION ABOUT HIMSELF: He was weak but must be strong and protect his mom and sister.

BILL'S INTERPRETATION ABOUT PEOPLE: People abandon you.

BILL'S SURVIVAL FORMULA: Be tough and strong.

When his dad died, at age 5 Bill became a man. He decided the world was a dangerous place and anyone might die or be hurt at any time, especially those he loved. Bill decided he would act tough, even though he felt weak and vulnerable. Although he was intelligent, Bill neglected his studies to work two jobs in between workout sessions at the gym. Bill became a police officer and enjoyed carrying his gun everywhere he went. Bill told himself that he was probably too dumb to have succeeded in school anyway.

Case Study #5

FACTS: At age 6, Paul went to his neighbor's house to play. His neighbor's older cousins beat him up and called him names. Paul ran home crying. His neighbor's grandmother said, "Paul was just being a baby."

PAUL'S INTERPRETATION ABOUT HIMSELF: He was a stupid, weak wimp.

PAUL'S INTERPRETATION ABOUT PEOPLE: People are mean and cruel and out to get you.

PAUL'S SURVIVAL FORMULA: Be smarter than everyone else.

Paul blamed himself for being stupid enough to visit his neighbor while his older cousins were there. He decided he went looking for trouble. When Paul took a beating at the hands of his neighbor's older cousins, he determined the world was a dangerous place and if he was to survive, it wouldn't be by defending himself physically. When the adult on the scene, his neighbor's grandmother, refused to defend him, he decided that no one else would protect him so he had better find a way to protect himself. He would have to outsmart his opponents. While his friends were outside playing, Paul spent his free time studying. He couldn't get enough knowledge. Paul became a perpetual student, continuing to take classes even after getting his Ph.D.

Case Study #6

FACTS: Mary wanted a Chatty Cathy doll for Christmas. She got a sweater and pants instead. Her mom said she had enough dolls and they couldn't afford wasting money.

MARY'S INTERPRETATION ABOUT HERSELF: She wasn't worth spending money on.

MARY'S INTERPRETATION ABOUT PEOPLE: People don't listen to your needs and don't care.

MARY'S INTERPRETATION ABOUT THE WORLD: There's scarcity of resources and not enough to go around.

MARY'S SURVIVAL FORMULA: Save money. Don't care.

Mary must have had a dozen dolls. But she really wanted this special one. When her mom gave her clothes instead, she felt that if she were good enough and her mom really loved her, she would have bought her the doll she wanted. Mary reasoned that her mom knew very well how much she wanted it but didn't listen and didn't care so she must have not been worth spending the money on. She decided since there wasn't enough to go around, only those who were worth it would be taken care of. Mary decided to work overtime and not spend her money frivolously. She would sacrifice and save for a rainy day when she might need it. Every time she considered treating herself to something nice, like a fancy restaurant dinner, she would reconsider. After all, she didn't want to waste money by spending it on herself. Besides, she didn't care anyway.

Case Study #7

FACTS: At age 18 months, Tom had to go to the hospital for a hernia operation. The nurses made Tom's mom leave as he was suspended in a harness over his hospital bed. Tom remembers screaming and pleading for his mom not to go. She went anyway.

TOM'S INTERPRETATION ABOUT HIMSELF: He is insignificant and not heard.

TOM'S INTERPRETATION ABOUT PEOPLE: People don't listen. People leave and abandon you.

TOM'S SURVIVAL FORMULA: Be quiet. You're not heard anyway.

At the age of 18 months, Tom stopped communicating. He had tried his best to be heard in a dire situation, but in spite of his yelling and screaming, his mom did not seem to hear him and left. Tom grew up as the quietest boy in his class. He rarely asked for things like most children do. He had decided it wouldn't make any difference. He wouldn't be heard. When Tom didn't receive those things he wanted (no one knew what he wanted as he never asked), he decided it was because no one loved him and no one listened to him. Even then, Tom remained quiet, thinking that if he spoke up and requested things, people would become angry with him and leave.

Case Study #8

FACTS: At age 7, Bobby was playing with matches in his bedroom and his model car caught fire. The flames from his model car spread to the curtains. Bobby panicked and vainly tried to put the fire out. By the time he ran to tell his parents, the fire had spread throughout the house. The house burned to the ground. Bobby's friend told him that his dad had called Bobby an evil brat. Bobby went to live with his grandmother for three years after that.

BOBBY'S INTERPRETATION ABOUT HIMSELF: He is evil and deserves bad things and to be punished. He is a throw-away.

BOBBY'S INTERPRETATION ABOUT PEOPLE: People suffer because of evil people like him.

BOBBY'S SURVIVAL FORMULA: To be good.

As he watched his house burn down, Bobby decided he would deserve whatever bad things happened to him for the rest of his life. When his mom and dad sent him to live with his grandmother, he reasoned it was because he was bad and they didn't love him or want him anymore. Bobby didn't comprehend that his parents' house was underinsured and it took them three years before they could provide him with another suitable home. At the age of 18, Bobby entered the seminary and later became a priest. Bobby spent the rest of his life attempting to contribute to society by working among the poor. However, no matter how hard he tried to make amends, Bobby was unable to rid himself of the guilt that originated from his mistake at age 7.

Case Study #9

FACTS: In first grade, Jane was afraid to ask the teacher for permission to go to the bathroom. She wet her pants. Her classmates laughed at her as a puddle formed underneath her desk. Her teacher made her stand in the corner as punishment for not speaking up and asking to go to the bathroom.

JANE'S INTERPRETATION ABOUT HERSELF: She was stupid.

JANE'S INTERPRETATION ABOUT PEOPLE: People are mean.

JANE'S SURVIVAL FORMULA: Play small. Don't risk. Try to remain invisible.

Jane had been humiliated twice that day. First when she wet her pants and then when she was made to stand in the corner. She decided that if she had been smart, she would have asked to go to the bathroom. She reasoned that she was humiliated because she was stupid and everyone knew she was stupid. She also decided people make fun of stupid people. Her conclusion was: The best that stupid people, like her, can do is try to make it through life without making a fool of themselves, as she had done in the past.

Case Study #10

FACTS: At age 7, Tommy had two chocolate bars he got for Halloween while trick-or-treating. One bar had peanuts. One was plain chocolate. Tommy didn't like peanuts, so he gave that candy bar to his 3-year-old brother, Nick. A peanut lodged in Nick's trachea, and he began to turn blue. Tommy ran yelling for his mom, who was able to dislodge the peanut. Tommy's mom scolded him for being so stupid as to give a 3-year-old a candy bar with nuts.

TOMMY'S INTERPRETATION ABOUT HIMSELF: He was selfish and stupid. He was bad and hurt people.

TOMMY'S INTERPRETATION ABOUT PEOPLE: People are fragile and easily damaged.

TOMMY'S SURVIVAL FORMULA: Avoid anything risky. Play safe.

The day Nick nearly choked to death was the day Tommy's spirit died. He could not forgive himself. He should have eaten the candy bar with nuts and given his brother the one without. How could he have been so stupid and selfish! Tommy's communication shut down from that day forward. He rarely spoke in groups or to strangers. He withheld his opinion and rarely contributed to others for fear of hurting them. He became an introvert in school and avoided social activities.

Wherever he went, Tom was known as the nice guy that no one ever heard a word from.

Case Study #11

FACTS: At 6, Mohammad moved from Pakistan with his parents to New York City. While walking home after his first day of school, three 10-year-old kids called him a "Muslim murderer" and repeatedly punched him in the stomach. Mohammad ran home crying. Mohammad's 15-year-old brother said, "That's just like Americans. No wonder we attacked them on September 11."

MOHAMMAD'S INTERPRETATION ABOUT HIMSELF: He was different, didn't belong and was hated.

MOHAMMAD'S INTERPRETATION ABOUT PEOPLE: People are hateful, cruel and unfair. They will hurt you if you don't hurt them first.

MOHAMMAD'S SURVIVAL FORMULA: Get others before they get you.

Mohammad's mood of rage first manifested that day he was

beaten. He decided Americans were hateful animals and vowed he would make them pay someday. As he grew older, other incidents of racial hatred further reinforced Mohammad's conviction that Americans were evil, hateful people. Mohammad decided he would get revenge on all Americans by becoming a terrorist martyr. "Let's see how they like suffering for a change," he thought.

Case Study #12

FACTS: When Bret was 7 years old, his dad died in the New York City World Trade Center attacks. Bret's mom cried herself to sleep almost every night for six months afterward.

BRET'S INTERPRETATION ABOUT HIMSELF: He was weak and helpless.

BRET'S INTERPRETATION ABOUT PEOPLE: Foreigners are evil and kill good people.

BRET'S SURVIVAL FORMULA: Hate and fear anyone different than you.

Bret decided that people who are different are evil and can't be trusted. Bret looked for opportunities to hate those he saw as different, especially those with different skin color and religious backgrounds. Bret became a bigot at age 7. He later joined a white supremacist gang and took part in vicious attacks on people of color.

Case Study #13

Facts: When Kathy was 3 years old, her parents divorced. Kathy went to live in an apartment with her mom.

Kathy's interpretation about herself: She was bad and unlovable and drove her dad away.

Kathy's interpretation about people: People leave. They don't love her. Her dad left because he didn't love her.

Kathy's survival formula: Leave others before they leave you.

At 3, Kathy decided that people want to leave her because she is not good enough and not worthy of love. Kathy has experienced dozens of broken relationships and four failed marriages. At the first sign of problems, Kathy either makes life with her partner so miserable that he leaves or she severs the relationship, proving that people leave and she is unlovable.

Case Study #14

Facts: Anthony preferred playing with his friends rather than doing household chores. On several occasions, starting when he was age 7, Anthony's mom got angry and called him fat and lazy.

Anthony's interpretation about himself: He was fat and must also be ugly, too. He was lazy and must be worthless, too.

ANTHONY'S INTERPRETATION ABOUT PEOPLE: People don't like him and he doesn't belong.

ANTHONY'S SURVIVAL FORMULA: Hide out. Don't let people know your weaknesses.

Anthony was a normal 7-year-old, loving life and wanting to play all day. His mom often became easily frustrated and took out her anger on her son. Growing up, Anthony seldom dated. He felt that no one would want to go out with such a useless ugly fat jerk. He became a recluse, hiding out in his apartment and venturing out into the world only when absolutely necessary. He often heard people talk about him behind his back. He knew it was because he was a loser.

Chapter 12

Reinterpret Your Past

Forgiveness means giving up your right to judge. Forgiving yourself takes the courage to release thinking you deserve to be punished. Doing so allows you to nurture your self-esteem.

Let's now explore the earliest incident you can remember that affected your perspective of yourself, others and the world. Take a few moments, close your eyes, relax and reflect back upon your early childhood. Go back as far in time as you can remember. Think about the early days in your family. Search your memory for any incident that left a significant impression upon you. Try to recall the event clearly. Who was present? Who said what? What did you say or do? Do not worry if you find it difficult to recall an early incident. Just do your best in remembering the earliest upset you can recall. Close your eyes now and reflect.

Did you recall a significant incident? If not, do not be concerned. Simply go back to the earliest upset you can remember. It is not critical that you necessarily remember the very first upset that influenced your self-image. We all have experienced subsequent upsets that have served to reinforce what we originally made up about ourselves. Choosing any one of these will suffice. So, close your eyes and think back to the earliest episode you can recall.

Unless this exercise is too disturbing for you, please do not read ahead until you have attempted to recall a time when you remember being angry, sad or scared and assumed something false about your value as a person.

Welcome back! Now that you have contemplated your past, please answer the following questions in as much detail as possible.

1. Describe the incident. What happened?
2. Separate the facts from what you felt and describe only the facts.
3. What was and is your predominant mood? (Some variation of anger, sadness or fear)
4. What assumption did you make about yourself?
5. What did you assume about other people?
6. What survival formula have you adopted to protect yourself from harm?
7. What negative interpretations have affected your self-esteem adversely?

And most importantly...

8. What new and empowering interpretations can you create about what happened?

These new interpretations have no mood attached. They do not make you feel angry, sad or afraid. They show compassion and empathy for yourself and others. They allow you to reframe the incident in such a way that you give yourself and others the benefit of the doubt. Your new interpretation does not blame yourself or anyone else for what happened. This may require you to adopt the perspective that everyone involved, you included, did the very best they knew how to do, in spite of their shortcomings. We are certainly not condoning any hurtful, abusive or criminal behavior. At the same time, your ability to forgive the participants for their mistakes and cast what transpired into a new and empathetic light will serve you in reclaiming your self-esteem. Now take the next step of the exercise:

9. In place of assuming something negative about yourself with respect to this incident, acknowledge yourself for some accomplishment that resulted from it (no matter how small or insignificant you might consider it to be). What was it?

Repeat the exercise with any other traumatic incidents you can recall. Notice any similarities in what you negatively interpreted about yourself or others. Reinterpret each incident to enhance your self-esteem. You will have succeeded in reframing each incident when you can reflect upon what happened without anger, sadness or fear and emerge from recalling the incident with a newfound self-respect.

Let's reinterpret each of the case studies we previously discussed in this manner.

Case Study #1:

FACTS: When 7-year-old Laura went to the eye doctor, he sexually molested her.

LAURA'S NEW INTERPRETATION ABOUT HERSELF: She was just an innocent little girl who ran into a sick man with a problem.

LAURA'S NEW INTERPRETATION ABOUT PEOPLE: People make mistakes. These mistakes do not have anything to do with our self-worth.

Case Study #2

FACTS: When John was 3 years old, his mom and dad brought home his new baby brother.

JOHN'S NEW INTERPRETATION ABOUT HIMSELF: He was so loved by his parents that they had another baby to be his best friend and companion.

JOHN'S NEW INTERPRETATION ABOUT PEOPLE: People are good-hearted and often do things to help others.

Case Study #3

FACTS: Linda's dad would get drunk and violent about once a week. When she was 9 years old, Linda's dad pushed her, she fell down the cellar steps and broke her arm.

LINDA'S NEW INTERPRETATION ABOUT HERSELF: She was lovable.

LINDA'S NEW INTERPRETATION ABOUT PEOPLE: Her dad had a drinking problem. He was a sick man and needed help controlling his disease. Her dad did not want to harm her or mean for her to fall and break her arm.

Case Study #4

FACTS: Bill's dad died in a car accident when Bill was 5 years old. His mom told him, "Bill, you're now the man of the family."

BILL'S NEW INTERPRETATION ABOUT HIMSELF: Bill is a fine person and his dad loved him dearly.

BILL'S NEW INTERPRETATION ABOUT PEOPLE: Accidents happen at times.

Case Study #5

FACTS: When Paul was 6, his neighbor's older cousins beat him up and called him names. When Paul ran home crying, his neighbor's grandmother called him a "baby."

PAUL'S NEW INTERPRETATION ABOUT HIMSELF: He was a perfectly normal little boy who was outsized by much larger, older kids.

PAUL'S NEW INTERPRETATION ABOUT PEOPLE: People have their own insecurities and do things to others to make themselves feel less insecure at times. They are hurting themselves and doing the best they know how. Grandma wasn't aware that Paul was actually hurt.

Case Study #6

FACTS: Mary wanted a Chatty Cathy doll for Christmas, but got clothes instead. Her mom said she had enough dolls and they couldn't afford wasting money.

MARY'S NEW INTERPRETATION ABOUT HERSELF: She was very much loved by her mom, who wanted the best for her. Giving her clothes was her mom's way of showing love by providing in the best way she knew how.

MARY'S NEW INTERPRETATION ABOUT PEOPLE: People act out of good intentions based upon how they see the world.

MARY'S NEW INTERPRETATION ABOUT THE WORLD: There's abundance in the world. Those who are creative can provide those they love with both necessities (clothes) and extravagances (toys).

Case Study #7

FACTS: At age 18 months, Tom went to the hospital for a hernia operation. The nurses made Tom's mom leave, even though Tom remembers screaming and pleading for her not to go.

TOM'S NEW INTERPRETATION ABOUT HIMSELF: He is valuable and greatly loved for his mom to have taken such good care of him.

TOM'S NEW INTERPRETATION ABOUT PEOPLE: His mom loved him and took great care of him. People love him and want what's best for him.

Case Study #8

FACTS: At age 7, Bobby was playing with matches in his bedroom and the house burned down. Bobby went to live with his grandmother for three years after that.

BOBBY'S NEW INTERPRETATION ABOUT HIMSELF: He was a curious, fun-loving little boy who unintentionally made a mistake.

BOBBY'S NEW INTERPRETATION ABOUT PEOPLE: People are resilient and not easily damaged.

Case Study #9

FACTS: In first grade, Jane wet her pants in class. Her classmates laughed at her and her teacher made her stand in the corner.

JANE'S NEW INTERPRETATION ABOUT HERSELF: She was a cute little girl who had an accident like little kids often do.
No big deal.

JANE'S NEW INTERPRETATION ABOUT PEOPLE: Her teacher was doing the best she knew how to do to teach her the skills she would find valuable in the world. This included learning the importance of making requests. People do the best they know how to based upon how they perceive the world.

Case Study #10

FACTS: At age 7, Tommy gave one of his Halloween candy bars to his 3-year-old brother, Nick. Nick choked on a peanut. Their mom dislodged the peanut, but she scolded Tommy for giving a 3-year-old a candy bar with nuts.

TOMMY'S NEW INTERPRETATION ABOUT HIMSELF: He was generous to share a candy bar with his brother.

TOMMY'S NEW INTERPRETATION ABOUT PEOPLE: People are hardy and quick to recover. His brother survived and did fine.

Case Study #11

FACTS: At 6, Mohammad moved from Pakistan with his parents to New York City. Walking home from school, he got beaten up and taunted. His older brother said, "That's just like Americans. No wonder we attacked them."

MOHAMMAD'S NEW INTERPRETATION ABOUT HIMSELF: He was a

great person. What the kids did had nothing to do with him. It was about them.

MOHAMMAD'S NEW INTERPRETATION ABOUT PEOPLE: Americans, like all the world's people, are human and do the best they know how consistent with how they perceive the world. Sometimes people are afraid and do foolish things because of their fear.

Case Study #12

FACTS: When Bret was 7, his dad died in the World Trade Center attacks.

BRET'S NEW INTERPRETATION ABOUT HIMSELF: He was a great person. His dad's death wasn't caused by anything he did.

BRET'S NEW INTERPRETATION ABOUT PEOPLE: People are good. Sometimes people are afraid and do foolish things because of their fear.

Case Study #13

FACTS: When Kathy was 3 years old, her parents divorced. Kathy went to live in an apartment with her mom.

KATHY'S NEW INTERPRETATION ABOUT HERSELF: She was a sweet and loveable little girl.

KATHY'S NEW INTERPRETATION ABOUT PEOPLE: Her dad's leaving had absolutely nothing to do with her. He still loved her very much. People love her and she is worthy of love.

Case Study #14

FACTS: Anthony preferred playing with his friends rather than doing household chores. His mom often got angry and called him fat and lazy.

ANTHONY'S NEW INTERPRETATION ABOUT HIMSELF: He was a fun-loving kid who naturally preferred playing to working, like most kids do. He enjoyed food. There was nothing wrong with this. He has the ability to take the weight off whenever he is ready to commit to a weight-loss program.

ANTHONY'S NEW INTERPRETATION ABOUT PEOPLE: People like him and accept him whenever he believes they will and acts according to this belief.

Chapter 13

Manage Your Interpretations Moment by Moment

Our success in managing interpretations is never permanently handled. We will always have a potential upset awaiting us to test our resolve.

You have done some work in identifying the possible source of your earliest faulty interpretations and how they helped erode your self-esteem. Now it's time to stress that these misinterpretations were not limited to only one, or to even just a few, traumatic early episodes. Our histories are all marked by innumerable situations where we have attributed a negative meaning to an event, causing us to become angry, sad or afraid. As we felt our mood engulf us, we adopted a negative interpretation about ourselves and the other people involved in the scene. This interpretation made us right and made someone else wrong. It allowed us to justify our behavior and dominate others or avoid being dominated. It was our human self-preservation mechanism at work to keep us safe from hurt and protected from possible future harm.

All our past experiences combine to influence how we will perceive our next stressful situation. The negative meanings we attribute to an upsetting event filter the way we perceive all subsequent events. The more we see things a certain way, the more likely we are to view future events that same way. As we look at the world through our filtered lenses, these filters influence what we see to a greater degree each time. The more we expect to see life in a certain way, the more it appears to do so. The images we perceive align themselves more and more with the filter we use. If we know the world to be an evil place, we see evil wherever we go. If we see it as good, that will be our experience. The stronger we emphasize our perceptions of these incidents, the more the future events will echo our prior results and match this expected image. Through our biased interpretations, we ensure that we get what we expect.

However, we have countless daily opportunities to break out of this vicious cycle simply by giving a different, emotion-free meaning to what current and future situations signify. When we take responsibility for reinterpreting the facts to create an empowering analysis of what happened, we are able to change the course of our lives. By generating implications that give the other person the benefit of the doubt, we can strengthen our bonds with others. We commit to living moment by moment from a non-judgmental perspective. The more we do so, the higher we elevate our opinions of others, our own self-opinions and nurture our growing sense of self-esteem.

Please remember that this does not mean that we condone abusive or inappropriate behavior. It simply means we recognize that everyone does the best they can, considering their limited perspective of the world.

With each opportunity to choose positive explanations of events, we have yet another chance to build our relationships and enhance our self-image. Doing so takes the courage and commitment to place more value in making life and relationships work than in feeding our thirst for our addictive mood. We must relinquish our need to beat ourselves up for being unworthy before we will see our personal stock soar.

We need to vigilantly reinterpret those daily occurrences where we used to routinely judge ourselves harshly. We will need to rigorously separate facts from our biased interpretations about others and their intentions. We will need to exercise the same rigor to end the cycle of judging ourselves severely. We do so by recognizing the falsehoods we construct to punish ourselves for being unworthy and unlovable. In a later chapter, we will discuss how to create a daily structure to support these aims.

Exercise

On a daily basis, notice your perceptions of events and conversations with others. Do you typically view the world from a positive, empowering perspective or from a negative, cynical one? Reinterpret each event or conversation from a positive point of view that is void of harsh self-judgment.

Chapter 14

Complete Your Past

Self-esteem starts with seeing things clearly. Building self-esteem comes from interpreting things to reflect an empowering truth.

Now that you have practiced reinterpreting your past with an empathetic new perspective, it's time to work through and put behind you any additional lingering issues that are draining your energy and sapping your self-esteem. Our lives are run by our incompletions. Unresolved experiences keep us from being fully present to life. When we are excessively preoccupied with our past mistakes, we trade our happiness, self-esteem and power for this obsession. Eighty percent of the process of reclaiming self-esteem involves putting the past behind us so that it no longer consumes our energy or attention and 20 percent entails designing your future. If negative, self-defeating interpretations of past events consume your attention and have you feeling bad about yourself, you will magnify and spread this overwhelming negative energy countless times.

Just as you have practiced reclaiming your self-esteem by reinterpreting your childhood upsets, you will need to follow the same process of separating facts from interpretations on a daily basis every time you encounter a new potential upset. By choosing to apply empowering meanings to each event, you will keep your relationships whole and build your self-image. As you go about your day, become proficient at recognizing the opportunity to manage your upsets. Release the emotions of anger, sadness or fear as they surface, and reinterpret what happened to recreate your future and reclaim your self-worth.

It is impossible to live fully in the present, welcoming each new experience moment by moment, if the baggage of unresolved issues and perspectives hinders our thoughts. Each day presents us with a new opportunity to resolve unfinished business and communicate responsibly, thus bringing us pride and peace.

Achieving completion means there is nothing more we feel compelled to say or do with respect to people or situations in our past. There are many means to accomplish this objective. Often, doing so involves nothing more than clarifying how our faulty misinterpretations about the past do not support our happiness and excellence. When we reinterpret past events, we are able to actually change history. The millions of memories we have about what happened in the past string together to make our life story. Most of these memories were fraught with the distorted meanings we gave to what happened. By altering our interpretations, our histories can be altered. Incidents that may have plagued us for years can disappear as if they never occurred once the emotional charge is taken from them. Disarming these painful memories allows us to reclaim self-esteem sacrificed by faulty analysis.

In some instances, we need to have a conversation with people from our past. Misunderstandings can be resolved by saying what has seemed true for you without needing to blame or make the other person wrong. This can do wonders for putting the past behind you and healing old wounds. Perhaps we may just need to say we are sorry for what transpired. Other situations may warrant that we forgive and tell the other person we love them.

Many times, completion can be achieved without reestablishing communication. There will be situations when reviving a relationship is undesirable. Perhaps it may be inappropriate or unwise to contact an ex-spouse or someone with a history of violence. Or, perhaps, we may wish to achieve completion with a deceased parent or family member. One way to do so is to write a letter to them that need not be mailed. In the letter, say everything you need to say in order to be whole. Withhold nothing. You might say,

- I am angry because...
- I am sad because...
- I am sorry for...

You might share your insights. Say anything and everything until you can't think of anything more to say. When you feel the release of energy, which accompanies completion, see if you can bring yourself to tell them that you love them or forgive them, or both. This does not mean that you condone their actions. You'll know when you are complete, as the need to change, fix or worry about something in your past will have vanished.

Exercise

Make a list of all of the people involved in your unresolved past events. What interpretations do you need to resolve? Devise an individual plan for each. Commit to doing whatever is appropriate to achieve completion over the next 30 days.

Chapter 15

The Power of Forgiveness

Forgiveness paves the way for self-esteem to flourish.

There is no more effective way to heal your past and encourage thriving relationships than by forgiving. It is critical that you begin this healing process by forgiving *yourself*. As we discussed in chapter five, the interpretation of failure does not serve us. We are all human and all make mistakes. The tragedy is not in making the mistake but in not having learned from it. And it's never too late to learn.

Part of the challenge is how we relate to mistakes and problems. In our culture, we have determined that problems are bad and that we shouldn't make mistakes. With this limiting view, we give very little room to take chances, aggressively pursue our dreams and honor our values. The concern of avoiding mistakes at all cost has us needlessly resign ourselves to a life that is less than ideal. If you can't afford to make a mistake, you won't have the freedom to grow, expand out of your comfort zone and achieve greatness. What if you adopted the perspective that everyone who lives makes mistakes and that the greatest mistake you can make is to have mistakes crush your spirit and steal your fervor for accessing the best that life has to offer? If we view mistakes as an essential component of our evolution, we will see that they actually support us to see things differently. As we continue to learn from them, our awareness increases and we are less likely to repeat these same mistakes.

From this point of view, powerful people focus not on avoiding problems and mistakes but on living their commitments instead. Embrace mistakes, learn from each one and look forward to the insights and gifts that are sure to come from experiencing future mistakes. By shifting our relationship to mistakes and overcoming our fear of avoiding problems, we can move on with our lives in a powerful manner. We can expect to make more mistakes, encounter many more problems and grow from each enriching experience. So, acknowledge yourself for having learned some extremely valuable lessons from your mistakes.

We all do the best we can to not only survive but to actually thrive as we go about our daily lives. We instinctively seek pleasure and avoid pain. Based upon the limited perspective we have as imperfect creatures, we will err from time to time. Please do not misunderstand. I am not condoning hurtful behavior. I am simply suggesting compassion for our human weaknesses. Adopt the attitude that you will continue to make mistakes until the day you draw your last breath. In the grand scheme of things, everything is important and nothing matters so much that we should choose the alternative to risking. This option is the death of our spirit and the resignation that comes with living in fear and playing not to lose instead of to win.

We are often our own harshest critics. When we judge ourselves to be bad and unworthy of love and life's greatest pleasures, we manifest a negative, destructive energy that ensures this be so. Our self-esteem suffers to the extent we maintain our right to punish ourselves for past weaknesses and mistakes. We attract the negative energy we put out into the world. By failing to forgive ourselves, we block the loving energy that cleanses our souls and allows us to share our greatest gift with others, the gift of being the best we can be.

By stubbornly keeping in place our critical self-judgments and the self-anger that accompanies them, we avoid responsibility for making our relationships stronger and our lives work most advantageously. Doing so allows us to shirk liability for communication. We stay angry with ourselves and keep active an unhealthy level of self-pity for our faults. This distracts us from getting on with our lives and cleaning up our mess. It's a lot more difficult to forgive and give up being a victim. Forgiving enables us to actively get about the business of making our lives and relationships flourish rather than keep alive the downward spiral of self-incrimination and blaming others. Making mistakes is part of the human condition. It has nothing to do with our worthiness as a person. It also has no bearing on the healthy unconditional self-acceptance essential to high self-esteem. Taking responsibility means committing to no longer act in a manner consistent with past mistakes, but to learn from them instead.

We hate those things about others that we hate most about ourselves. Forgiving ourselves is the first step in clearing the way to forgive others. By forgiving yourself, the toxic resentment that consumes your spirit and destroys self-esteem will give way to the self-love that fosters forgiving and loving others.

Waiting for others to initiate reconciliation will not support your relationships, health or self-image. Healing your past will come from the empathy you initiate by putting yourself in the other person's world and understanding why he may have acted as he did. By being the first to forgive others, you pave a new road to a future based upon love rather than anger. Remember that anger results from our interpretations about what was done, not the actions themselves. Forgiving will make you the champion and designer of your future self, a self you can feel good about.

There may be some people who *you* have hurt or wronged. Look to see if there is anything you can do to make amends for hurting them with past behavior. Clean up misspoken words and acknowledge mistakes. Acknowledge the casual promises that you blew off as being unimportant. Offer a sincere apology if you have erred and commit to make things right and repair the damaged relationship, if possible. Your reparation should be appropriate for the damage you caused and directed at the person harmed. When you actively accept responsibility for your part in failed communication or a wounded relationship, you act with the courage to make things right. This commitment blazes a trail to a new way of being.

When you apologize for past mistakes and take appropriate action to clean up the mess created, you take responsibility for your part by giving a 100 percent effort toward healing the relationship. However the other person chooses to respond, take comfort in knowing you have done whatever you could to repair the harm. It will support you to be committed to healing the relationship without an attachment to having the other person respond in kind. By showing a willingness to repair the situation to the best of your ability, you have done your part to initiate a healing of the relationship. Keep the door open to communication, congratulate yourself for courageously taking action in the direction of completion and get on with your life.

When you have done everything you can to right a past indiscretion, it will not support you to continue to berate yourself about what was done. We all make mistakes. All we can ask of ourselves is to continue to learn from our actions, commit to honoring others and take responsibility for being the person we declare ourselves to be. Again, this does not excuse hurtful or wrongful action. It simply means acting from love once you see that you have caused another pain or loss.

With this foundation of love, you free yourself to declare who you are to the world. Resentment no longer dictates your reactions. The attachment to making yourself right and others wrong will fade and a commitment to deliberately designing the person you are will be possible. Miracles will manifest and your self-image will soar.

Exercise

List all the items that you have not yet forgiven yourself and others for. Create a plan to clean up any misspoken words, acknowledge mistakes and apologize for any errors you may have made. For those deceased or those you cannot or choose not to achieve completion with in person, write a letter expressing your thoughts, emotions and forgiveness. Mailing the letter is optional.

Chapter 16

The Importance of Gratitude

I felt bad about not having new shoes until I saw the person who didn't have any feet.
— Unknown

So we've realized that the faulty interpretations we give to what happens to us in life damage our self-esteem and inhibit our magnificence. We take what someone says or does and almost automatically put a negative spin on it. We interpret comments and events as being aimed at us personally and to mean we are less worthy and not good enough to deserve the best life has to offer. Rather than dwelling on thoughts that champion our excellence or support our happiness, we accept the degrading message – sometimes internally from Chip, sometimes from others – that we lack what it takes to be successful, prosperous, joyful, involved in rewarding relationships and proud of who we are. As a result, we feel sorry for ourselves.

We can shift our attention from this quagmire of self-pity, partly by gratefully focusing on our blessings. Gratitude helps us concentrate on our strengths rather than our weaknesses so we can make the most of the gifts we are blessed with. Why waste time accentuating our flaws? When we see the world through grateful eyes, we can direct our attention toward contributing to others, expanding our horizons and taking profitable risks, as opposed to wallowing in self-pity and shrinking from fully realizing our potential.

Grateful people live optimistically. Their glasses are always half full, not half empty, and they're not afraid to keep drinking because they know the glass will be filled again. They make the most of what they have been given. They have decided to be excellent persons and take responsibility for developing any missing areas that would contribute to this excellence. Having gratitude takes the focus off oneself. It creates an ever-replenishing wellspring of positive energy that allows one to contribute to others. This continual commitment to contribution nurtures self-esteem.

It is difficult to feel bad about yourself when you surround yourself with people who are grateful for your contribution to them. If you find yourself surrounded by cynical, negative people who tend to erode your self-esteem, commit to widening your circle of friends and contacts to include people who appreciate your company and value the contribution you make to their lives just by being you. Decide now to spend more time with people who nurture your essential self by treating you as a worthy friend and equal. As you become more in touch with your gifts and further develop your interests, seek out individuals who share these interests and appreciate your value. Do not fall into the trap of minimizing your value to others. Seek out opportunities to contribute to others. No contribution is too small. Even a kind word or a friendly smile can brighten someone's day. As you develop the gift of friendship, you and they will grow in gratitude for the blessings you bring to each other's lives.

Similarly, open yourself up to contributions from others. We cannot fully give of ourselves if we are reluctant to receive from others. Allow people to experience the gift of contributing to you. Acknowledge their generosity and gladly welcome the value they have shared with you. Notice how allowing them to support you in some way has given them the gift of self-esteem as well.

Daily practice giving and receiving gratitude at every possible opportunity. The more you become consciously aware of the many people and things you have in your life for which you can be grateful, the easier it will be to feel an ever-expanding sense of gratitude and worthiness.

Exercise

Decide to be grateful. Make a list of all the reasons you have to be grateful. Before going to bed each night, record those blessings for which you have decided to be grateful. List at least five. Daily decide to contribute to someone who might benefit from your support. Each day acknowledge yourself and your value for your contribution to someone else. Don't dismiss anything as being too small. Recall the people who have contributed to you or supported you today and plan to acknowledge them with gratitude.

Section Two:
Assess Your Present

Chapter 17

Do a Values Inventory

Responsibility starts with a commitment to honor your values.

Let's begin our assessment of your level of emotional fulfillment by discussing the concept of values. It is helpful for us to speak in terms of three types of values: key values, obligatory values and up-and-coming values.

The failure to honor your own most important or key values perpetuates low self-esteem. These values make up the essence of who we are. When we live in harmony with them, we nurture our spirits and elevate our own high regard. Key values exist at the very center of our being. When they are violated, life becomes a struggle. When they are dishonored, we become angry, our communication breaks down and relationships suffer. We feel resentful toward others and bad about ourselves.

When we honor these key values, we are most happy and life is most meaningful. Clarifying what our key values are supports us in directing our lives toward their pursuit. By recognizing your most important values, you can design your actions to be consistent with their realization.

Look at some examples of the many key values that form the foundation for self-esteem:

- Safety
- Happiness
- Belonging
- Freedom
- Intimacy
- Communication
- Abundance
- Love
- Security
- Peace
- Adventure
- Integrity
- Respect

Consider now the following questions:

- Which of your key values do you feel you cannot happily live without?
- Which values are not being fully honored?
- How does this affect your vitality and self-image?
- What will you put into place within the next 30 days to begin to honor these essential components that nourish your spirit?
- Name three people you will ask to support you in honoring these values.
- What specific actions will you immediately take toward this goal?

Let's turn our attention now to the concept of obligatory values. These values are not really your own but are forced upon you by others. We refer to these as "shoulds."

Society, your family, friends or others who believe they know how you should act impose obligatory values. Such "shoulds" go against your wishes, goals and desires. They do not support you to make your own decisions that contribute to your happiness. They are based upon standards that others have set regarding right and wrong or rules of acceptable behavior. You unwillingly follow such values because you feel you are forced or coerced into doing so. Any place you find yourself with a "should" is a place you will find yourself suffering. This is not to say that the principles behind these forced values are not necessarily worthwhile or possessing merit. However, if you did not have guilt or fear some negative result or retribution, you would not choose to pursue these values on your own. Obligatory values do not empower or contribute to your happiness as key values do. There will be times when they support your goals or intentions and other times when the more positive outcomes that accompany violating them outweigh the negative consequences of blindly obeying them.

An example might be the statement, "You should never tell a lie." There will be many times when this principle will serve you well. But what if telling a lie is necessary to protect a loved one or keep a pleasant surprise from being leaked? The inherent problem with obligatory values is that they lack the flexibility necessary to make life work optimally at times.

Growing up a Catholic in the 1950's and 60's meant complying with the obligatory value, "You shouldn't eat meat on Friday." The reasoning behind this rule involved the value of sacrificing for a higher good. However, as a 6-year-old, I clearly recall being faced with the dilemma of an aunt buying me a hotdog for my lunch on Friday. Knowing that it also had been stressed that, "It's a sin to waste food," I was faced with the lose-lose options of either eating meat on Friday or wasting food and going hungry. No matter which decision I made, it carried the consequences of doing something wrong and being bad! This is one problem with obligatory values. They do not empower happiness or allow for flexibility in judgment regarding what serves the person best in a particular situation.

Do not confuse obligatory values with a moral code. We are not saying that these behaviors are bad or encouraging situational ethics. In fact, many of the following concepts are founded upon sound principles and often conveyed with good intentions. The underlying value may not be at fault so much as the overwhelming sense of obligation that was used to inculcate it. If the value is not your own value, but one that has been dictated to you by another, it is defined as an obligatory value. Here are some of the typical obligatory values you may have experienced:

- **Cleanliness**
  "You should clean up your room and do your chores."

  "Cleanliness is next to godliness!"

  "You shouldn't get dirty while playing."

- **Scarcity**
  "Don't be wasteful. Money doesn't grow on trees."

  "Eat all the food on your plate. People are starving in Africa!"

  "Shut off the lights. Do you think I own shares in the electric company?"

- **Obligation**

  "You should visit your elderly relatives."

  "You will go to medical school and become a doctor."

  "That's not how a good wife, husband, child, parent acts."

  "You should go to church every Sunday."

  "Marriage should be forever. You shouldn't get divorced."

  "You should provide for your family the same way I provided for you."

- **Respect**

  "Respect your elders, no matter what they say."

  "Children should be seen and not heard."

  "A promise is a promise and should never be broken."

  "Married people shouldn't act that way."

- **Goodness**

  "Good boys and girls do what they are told."

  "Ladies don't speak that way to others."

  "Good parents love all their children alike."

  "Fat people aren't attractive."

- **Generosity**

  "Good children share their toys."

  "You should give a percentage of your income to charity."

"You should volunteer your time."

"You should think of others before yourself."

- **Proper actions**
  "Grown men don't cry or show their emotions."

  "That's not very ladylike."

  "Stop being sad (or angry or afraid)."

  "Idleness is the devil's workshop. You should be busy."

  "Hard work never hurt anyone."

- **Worthiness**
  "If you were more _________, you wouldn't have this problem."

  "You should only marry a doctor, professional person, member of your same race, religion, etc."

  "You should know the answer."

  "You should be successful."

When you were a child, society and your parents instilled within you many of these obligatory values. They said or implied that you were good when you followed the rules and bad when you broke them. They collapsed the moral interpretations of good and bad with guidelines meant to support you in making your life work. Their intentions were honorable. They wanted you to learn the tools you would need to live a productive, successful and structured life. However, the consequences of breaking the rules were, all too often, the interpretation that you were bad. What was set up to support your life to be productive, effective and happy produced the exact opposite result. It diminished your self-esteem a little more each time you failed to live up to the restrictive expectations imposed.

You may have followed this same pattern and instilled many of these shoulds into your own children. Despite the best of intentions, these forced values can result in the decision that "I am bad" because I have not followed the rules.

People use force, coercion and intimidation to keep obligatory values in place. Obligatory values can dominate us and rob us of our free will because of the inflexibility with which they are often presented. We resent the pressure to conform. We also feel guilt if we violate them. Our self-esteem suffers either way.

Take a few moments now and reflect upon the following questions:

- What obligatory values did you grow up with?
- Which ones are still in place today? Where do you feel guilty or torn between what you should do and what you want to do?
- How do these forced values erode your self-esteem?
- Create an empowering interpretation to explain why others may have pushed each of these values upon you.
- Which obligatory values will you discard as no longer serving your happiness and the person you have decided to be?

- Which ones support your self-image and serve you to keep in place?
- Create a new interpretation to replace any previous ones that had you labeled as bad or wrong if you failed to comply with these values. Remind yourself of this new interpretation each time you judge yourself harshly for violating this obligatory value.
- What do you need to put into place to eliminate unwanted obligations that damage your self-esteem?
- By what date will you take these actions?
- Record your insights in your journal. (More on journaling later.)

Many times, our inner struggle stems from the conflict between what we want to do and what we should do "if we were good or responsible." We live in a state of either/or. Either we can do our homework or go outside to play. Either we can watch the game or spend time with the kids. Either we can work hard or take the day off.

What we often miss is the possibility of doing both. If we can train ourselves to look outside the box and consider and/both as a possible solution to our dilemma, instead of either/or, often we can have the best of both worlds.

Decide today to honor your own values and exercise your right to choose your actions. Of course, all actions bring with them consequences. Be clear about what the short- and long-term consequences are of rejecting any obligatory values. What we resist we also keep in place. Decide to accept full responsibility for your choices.

Let's now discuss the concept of up-and-coming values. Like the layers of an onion, as certain basic key values become honored, other values show up as important and beg to be honored.

We all need a reserve to protect us from the chaos and stresses of life. Without such a reserve, our daily preoccupations are spent in an effort to survive and fight off threats. For example, to a homeless person, key values might be safety and security. Until these are honored, other up-and-coming values such as creativity, adventure, wealth and other values not essential for survival cannot even be considered.

The same concept applies to those lacking self-esteem. As we grow in self-esteem, we see new and exciting possibilities open up for our lives. It's as though we are riding up a tall skyscraper in a glass elevator with each floor representing a higher degree of self-esteem. When we are at ground level, all we can see as we look outside the elevator window is the brick wall in front of us. As our self-esteem grows, so does our perspective with respect to our up-and-coming values. The higher the elevator climbs, the more expansive our vista and the more beautiful the world around us appears. As our self-image soars to the height of the penthouse suite, we can hardly believe that our ability to see clearly was once so restricted.

As your self-esteem grows in the coming months and years, take time to reflect upon the new up-and-coming values that you find waiting to be honored as your life enriches.

Chapter 18

Take Personal Inventory: Put Closure on Your Past and Tend to Unfinished Business

You can't live powerfully in the present if your mind is on the past.

As we have discussed, those past events you have not yet successfully put behind you continually consume your attention. Decide now to put closure on those experiences that drain your energy, distract your attention and steal your power. Closing the past will elevate your self-esteem by enabling you to act deliberately in the present while meeting the future with the strength your full attention will provide.

If you find yourself preoccupied with the past, you will be unable to respond to new possibilities with the velocity that comes from being fully present to life. Tend to any unresolved business, and stresses from these past events will no longer plague you as they compete for your attention.

By putting closure on these items, you will minimize the potential for unwelcome shocks that drain your effectiveness and hamper your self-esteem. Cleaning up these items translates into accepting responsibility for doing whatever it takes to deal with any challenges that might threaten your vision for the future. This will result in a mental, physical or spiritual cushion to safeguard against life's problems.

Resolving and putting your past incompletions behind you will make you aware of all areas where you feel stunted or lacking. If you often focus your energy on areas where you feel you don't measure up, you will not be able to pay full attention to making your life work best in the here and now.

Carefully ponder the following list and check off all items that apply. Add any that you feel would complete your list in each category.

Health, Appearance and Personality

- I am happy with my appearance.
- I have no lingering physical problems or untreated chronic conditions.
- I went for a physical exam recently.
- My dental health is cared for and my dental appearance is good.
- I am not taking drugs or abusing alcohol.
- I do not smoke or otherwise abuse my body.
- I look my best.
- I keep my hair, nails and appearance neat and attractive.
- I brush and floss my teeth regularly.
- My eyes have been checked recently, and my vision is good or has been corrected with eyeglasses or contact lenses.
- I dress neatly, smell good and make a good impression.
- My home, office and car accurately reflect who I am.
- I have no unhealthy habits.
- I typically see the glass as half-full.
- I keep my weight at a steady, healthful range.

- I am relaxed, not anxious or nervous.
- I am creative and imaginative.
- I have a good sense of humor.
- I do not speak poorly of myself and do not tolerate others doing so.
- I experience few upsets on a daily basis.
- My life is purposeful and organized.
- I am not easily stressed out.
- I take care of all aspects of my health.
- Others consider me competent.
- I expect life will always get better and better.
- Other items:

____

____

____

Wealth, Finances, Career, and Occupation

- I save a significant portion of my earnings weekly or monthly.
- I pay off my credit cards in full monthly.
- I pay my taxes and file my returns on time.
- I have adequate insurance to protect against unfortunate losses or illnesses.
- My business is in good financial order.
- My colleagues respect me at work.
- I do not overwork on a regular basis or to the point of extreme absorption of my personal time.
- All my debts are manageable and current.
- My work is fulfilling and I love what I do.
- I am honest, likeable and trustworthy.

- People respect my abilities.
- I do not use people for my own benefit and at their expense.
- My coworkers know that I am dependable.
- People trust my judgment and readily accept my advice.
- I determine my own destiny.
- I enjoy a new challenge and willingly accept healthy risks.
- I have not settled for a job that frustrates or limits me.
- I greet each day with eager anticipation and love what I do.
- I delegate to others those tasks I need not do myself.
- Other items:

  ____

  ____

  ____

Relationships

- I make friends easily and have many close friends.
- My relationships are mutually fulfilling.
- I associate with people who I proudly call my friends.
- I feel comfortable in most social situations.
- I am good at making and keeping commitments.
- I have no toxic relationships.
- I do not overly depend upon any person.
- I trust others and they trust me.
- I reach my appointments on time.
- My life is gossip-free.
- Others would say I am not judgmental.
- I am not withholding communication or love in any of my relationships.

- I respect the values of others and they respect mine.
- My relationships are authentic, warm and truthful.
- I have a close and intimate relationship with my spouse or partner.
- I have a healthy attitude about sex. I think others find me sexually attractive and am not afraid to express my sexuality.
- Others would call me a good communicator and listener.
- I enjoy time with my friends in addition to sharing friends with my spouse or partner.
- I have forgiven everyone who has hurt me.
- I am not consumed by guilt.
- People would say I am easygoing and seldom moody.
- I am not displaying any abusive behavior.
- I do not live in hope that, by chance, someday I will meet the right person who will make my life right.
- I have no problem asking to have my needs met.
- I take responsibility for making every aspect of my life work optimally.
- Other items:

____

____

____

Family

- I love my family, they love me and we tell each other so regularly.
- I hold no unresolved anger toward any family member.
- All my family legal and financial records are in order.
- I have forgiven everyone who has hurt me.

- I have apologized to anyone who I have hurt and have done all I can to repair the relationship.
- I regularly make time to connect with my family.
- I do not gossip or allow for unhealthy behavior in my family, as a co-conspirator.
- Other items:

  ____

  ____

  ____

Personal and/or Spiritual Development

- I take time for my personal development.
- I defined a clear, written vision for my life and read it daily.
- I have a powerful relationship with God.
- I am confident in my self-worth.
- I regularly work with a life and/or business coach.
- I don't simply tolerate life but live it to the fullest.
- I regularly read and listen to material that nurtures my greatness and inspires me.
- I am knowledgeable about current events.
- I learn something new everyday.
- I trust and act upon my intuition.
- I am in touch with my values and my life expresses them fully.
- I am aware of my gifts and contribute them freely.
- I expect my life to work optimally and am committed to making it happen.
- I tell the truth.
- The legacy I will leave the world is ____________.

- Other items:

____

____

____

Recreation and Fun

- I have fun with other people at least weekly.
- I have hobbies that I find rewarding.
- I know what makes me happy and do it often.
- Others consider me to be a fun person.
- I balance work with play.
- I take time just for me.
- My pets are in good health, well-groomed and cared for.
- Other items:

____

____

____

The intent of the above exercise is not to point out weaknesses or berate you for them. Everyone has strengths, areas that can be developed and attitudes that can be changed to support happiness and excellence.

Exercise

Now that you have taken your personal inventory, create a preliminary list of all items you will decide to work upon. Make note of those items that can be specifically addressed by detailed actions. You will further refine this list in Chapter 19. You will also incorporate these elements into your vision and the action plan we will create together in Chapter 25.

Prioritize your list so you can set specific deadlines for addressing each as you craft your plan of action. Separate what is really so from the meanings you have attributed to each quality that cause your self-esteem to plummet.

As you learn to accentuate your strengths and reframe your weaknesses to take a less prominent role in your overall self-image, your harsh self-judgment will lessen and your self-love will increase.

Chapter 19

Assess Your Strengths and Weaknesses

Failure is an interpretation that does not support self-esteem. Reinterpret your "failed" experiences to acknowledge your insights, growth and accomplishments. Rather than run from failure, embrace it, learn from it and create so much of it that it becomes a big "so what!" Only those willing to risk failure can accomplish great things.

You have done some work to resolve your past, to identify your key values and to take a personal inventory. Now it's time to further evaluate your strengths and weaknesses. I am not giving you permission to beat yourself up! In fact, commit now to forever give up the right to invalidate yourself. Simply recognize when you are judging yourself harshly and return to your commitment to give yourself a break and love yourself. It will mean creating an interpretation that keeps you whole and properly reflects your self-worth.

We all have gifts. The trouble often is that we are not fully in touch with what these gifts are. What are you known for? What are you passionate about? When are you most alive or having fun? To uncover all your gifts, you may need to ask others for feedback about what they see them to be. Record all your strengths and gifts on several index cards and keep them where you will see them. Perhaps, keep one by your phone, one on your bathroom mirror, one in your car and one wherever you are most likely to be reminded of the need to revisit these qualities. As you realize additional assets, add them to your list. As you become more in touch with your magnificence, your list will grow.

Let's turn now to your weaknesses. Consider past mistakes as learning opportunities and weaknesses as simply qualities that can be changed, areas of potential you have yet to develop. Minimize the importance of those that can't be altered by realizing how insignificant they are in comparison to your strengths. Reflect upon your health, occupation, finances, relationships, family, personal or spiritual development, recreation and fun. In each area, what is missing that, if put into place, would enhance your happiness, life-style, relationships and self-esteem? For some areas, you will readily know what you need to do to improve your life. For others, you may need the help of a coach to design a plan to address what may be missing. Consider any absent areas similar to a weak muscle that has been in a cast for six weeks. The cast has now been removed, and you will deliberately focus on exercising the muscle to strengthen it with use and loving attention.

Please review the following list of potential qualities you might consider developing to maximize your effectiveness with people and further enhance self-esteem.

Qualities to Support Your Excellence

- Being calm and centered
- Not reacting
- Being organized and focused
- Being at peace
- Having genuine humility
- Choosing interpretations that support or empower you
- Having greater physical energy
- Working on your health and appearance
- Having integrity

- Exuding charisma
- Showing confidence
- Being an inspiration to yourself and others
- Allowing yourself to be vulnerable when appropriate
- Showing emotion
- Not showing emotion when it does not serve you
- Being sensitive
- Being consistent or persistent
- Being coachable or teachable
- Being happy
- Having a good self-image
- Trusting your intuition
- Developing empathy
- Being self-motivated
- Being able to make and keep commitments
- Being able to be told anything without reacting
- Being a good listener
- Being able to make the most of any situation
- Being able to have fun
- Coming across authentically to others
- Having discipline
- Willing to sacrifice for the future
- Speaking from the heart
- Living your vision
- Supporting others
- Championing others to excellence
- Exuding enthusiasm
- Being inspirational
- Being vulnerable
- Having compassion
- Possessing a positive attitude
- Choosing to have positive expectations
- Communicating effectively

You might choose to develop the following qualities in relation to others:

- Listening for mutuality or common ground
- Listening for what others have to contribute to you
- Listening for opportunities to strengthen your relationship (as opposed to listening to be offended)
- Being able to bond with others
- Possessing the ability to work well in partnership
- Being happy to serve
- Being willing to contribute
- Not interrupting
- Being a team player

Adapted from "The Power to Succeed: 30 Principles for Powerful Living" by Dr. Joe Rubino © 2002.

Exercise

Create a list of your strengths and gifts. Identify your weaknesses. Which of these can be strengthened and developed? From the list above, select the top five qualities that will support your happiness, power and effectiveness.

Chapter 20

Reprogram Your Subconscious Mind

He is rich or poor according to what he is, not according to what he has.
— Henry Ward Beecher

With the prior exercises in mind, make a list of all the qualities and values that the new, reinvented you will embody. These qualities include both current assets as well as attributes you've identified that need strengthening. State these qualities and values in a positive manner. For example, say "happy" instead of "not angry," "easygoing" instead of "not difficult," "loving" instead of "not hateful."

Your list might look something like this:

My New Qualities and Values

I am:
- Secure
- Self-confident
- Loving
- Loved
- Forgiving
- Charismatic
- Courageous
- Attractive

A good listener
Self-motivated
Authentic
Enthusiastic
Empathetic
Social
Someone who belongs
Inspiring
Happy
A great friend
A contributor
Committed
Easygoing
I listen for value
I strengthen relationships

List those qualities that would best represent the ideal you, a magnificent and secure person with high self-esteem. Now, take the qualities from your list and group them together into sentences. These will serve as your new, empowering affirmations that will reprogram your thoughts. For example, if your qualities were those listed above, your affirmations might be:

I am a self-confident and loving person.
I am secure in my value as a great friend
and I am loved by many.
I belong and fit in beautifully wherever I go.
I forgive others and myself for all faults
and shortcomings.
I am happy, social, easygoing and fun to be around.
I inspire others with my courage and authenticity.

I am attractive, charismatic and well-groomed.
I am a good listener.
I listen for value in every conversation.
I am easygoing and let little bother me.
I strengthen my relationships.
I am self-motivated and enthusiastic.
I empathize with the other person.
I frequently contribute my gifts to others.
I acknowledge my value and regularly
do nice things for myself.

Exercise

Create your own list of the qualities and values embodied by the new, reinvented you. Group related qualities into complete sentences – your own personal affirmations. Type these affirmations on heavy stock or index cards and place them throughout your home and office at key points where you'll see them daily. Take a few minutes at least three times a day to read and focus upon the healing energy of these affirmations. Better yet, read your new affirmations into a tape recorder. Play back your tape several times daily while closing your eyes and focusing on the feeling you get when you are these traits. For an additional, even more effective means of delivering affirmations directly to your subconscious, I recommend Dr. Eldon Taylor's subliminal audio, "Soaring Self-esteem."

A Note About the Power of Subliminal Affirmations

Reprogramming the subconscious mind has been the life work of Dr. Eldon Taylor. The patented and scientifically proven technology he developed is called InnerTalk®. His work has influenced the lives of millions of people worldwide and has been featured on the Discovery Channel. According to Dr. Taylor, the conscious mind can only guess at what is in the subconscious mind and its best guess comes by listening to one's own self talk. This stream of consciousness often reveals our innermost fears, doubts, worries and defense strategies-many of which have become outmoded in our maturity or simply are self defeating in nature. He praises reinventing the self to consciously make the decision with respect to who you are and what your path or purpose in life is. To do this, Dr. Taylor strongly urges the inclusion of affirmations delivered directly to the subconscious, so that the mind's "conscious sentry" cannot negate or cancel their positive value.

Think for a minute – you want to reinvent yourself and be successful and prosperous. To do that, how much income will you make this year? Let's say that you decide on one million dollars. Don't laugh or balk – just think to yourself, "I will make one million dollars this year!" Think this sincerely and see if you get any back talk from your subconscious. Do you hear things like, "Sure, what are you going to do-rob a bank?" Now imagine Bill Gates thinking of the money that he will earn this year. Do you think he believes that it will be less than $1 million? No – not too likely for the wealthiest man in the world. Yet, you intuitively know that you cannot do anything that you do not believe is possible.

Dr. Taylor's InnerTalk® technology exists for precisely this reason – to impact your belief in yourself. It dialogues through a patented method directly with the subconscious, and the affirmations enter the stream of consciousness without intercession or conscious mitigation. Soon the affirmations accumulate in such a way as to become your own thoughts, your own beliefs. It's not someone else telling you something from the outside in. No, this comes from the inside out. This tool is a powerful technological advance that can support your other efforts at reclaiming your magnificence. You still must do the doing, but it's truly a technological breakthrough that can make that reinvention happen with greater acceleration! For this reason, I recommend Dr. Taylor's "Soaring Self-Esteem" to augment this book's work. To learn more about this technology, visit www.progressiveawareness.com.

Chapter 21

Create a Structure to Develop Those Qualities You Identify as Missing

Feeling sorry for people keeps them small and damages their self-esteem. People are magnificent. Holding them so champions them and raises their self-esteem.

From the list of qualities you developed in the previous exercise, select the top five missing qualities that, if strengthened and developed, would contribute most to your self-esteem.

Begin to work on your health and appearance, if these areas are not up to your expectations. Decide to go back to school to develop a valuable skill or new profession if that's what's needed. If fun or rewarding relationships are missing, focus on activities that meet these needs. If you are so busy taking care of the needs of others, make a list of your own priorities as a person worthy of special attention and pampered care.

Notice how often you feel sorry for yourself. If this is a common challenge, get out into the world and apply your focus upon a worthwhile goal or cause that pulls you out of your rut. Interacting with others and taking the focus off you will do wonders for your emotional state and positive new direction.

Maybe you will work on becoming a better listener. This could mean listening patiently and not interrupting. Perhaps you will listen for something of value that might contribute to your life in whatever is said, regardless of the style of the person presenting it. Or, listen for the "gold" instead of the "dirt" in a conversation. All of these empowered listening attitudes will support your relationships, allow others to be heard and reward you with an elevated self-image as your communications skills improve.

Let's speak now about listening to others when the heat is on, like during an argument or confrontation. These are the times when new communication tools are most critical to strengthen your self-esteem. In times of stress, put yourself into the other person's world and ask yourself the question, "What could this person be thinking for her to act as she does?" If you are not quite sure what she might be thinking, create an interpretation that helps you empathize with her. Doing so will provide you with the insights to better understand that people do the best they can according to how they view the world. Although their actions may often seem personally offensive, they are entranced in their own world and haven't taken time to consider how their words or acts affect you or others.

Working on not being personally offended by what others say or do will help rebuild your self-image. All too often, we take things personally and our self-esteem suffers. By creating the space for people to be whoever they are with all their faults and frailties, you allow them to do whatever they do without implying anything negative about you. By releasing your need to control who they are or how they act, you will generate harmony and strengthen esteem. Freedom always comes when you release the desire to dominate or control others and don't emotionally attach yourself to the outcome.

Exercise

Once you have identified these first five qualities to develop, practice the following structures to support your success.

1. *Take some specific daily action that will help you develop each trait.*
2. *At the end of the day, rate yourself on a scale from 1 to 10 with respect to how well you embodied each quality.*
3. *Keep a daily journal describing what worked that day to develop each characteristic. Also note what was missing that, if put into place, would better serve your objective.*
4. *Request the support of family members and friends in championing you to develop your chosen traits.*

Section Three:
Design Your Future

Chapter 22

Keep a Daily Journal

People hate being dominated. If they don't have the freedom to say no, they don't have the freedom to say yes. Empower them with choices and watch their self-esteem increase.

From this moment forward, I invite you to live your life deliberately. By this, I mean that you begin to analyze who you are being daily that either supports your happiness, relationships and self-esteem or that detracts from them. Become vigilant to negative self-talk moment by moment as you go about your day. Your self-esteem will increase to the extent you can first recognize when Chip is speaking his nonsense and then reinterpret each thought and situation in a way that champions your self-image. One tool to support you in your deliberate approach is a daily journal. A journal can be a spiral-bound notebook or hardcover log made expressly for this purpose. Choose your journal book with the expectation that you will treasure it for life as one of many volumes permitting you to reflect back on your personal development progress.

Your journal can be used to record the exercises suggested in this book. It is also valuable for noting any observations, including your daily commitments, challenges, insights and breakthroughs (those aha! experiences).

Begin by recording your observations to the following as you go about your day:

- Catch yourself in negative self-talk.
- Distinguish what is really so from the damaging story you decided about yourself.
- Note whenever you demand perfection or blame yourself for things that are not your fault or beyond your control.
- Record any assumptions that others are judging you as harshly as you judge yourself. Separate out exactly what they said from what you think they meant that has you berating yourself. Create a new, empowering interpretation that gives you the benefit of the doubt.
- When you hear negative self-talk, ask yourself, "Is it possible that I am distorting what actually happened?
- Are you taking what others say personally? What other interpretation can you apply to these comments, assuming they are not directed at you?
- Are you comparing yourself to others unfavorably? How can you focus on your strengths instead? Acknowledge yourself for a positive trait every time you entertain a negative thought.

At the end of each day, also record your insights to the questions below:

- Did my thoughts and actions today reflect my values and commitments and contribute to building my growing self-esteem?
- What worked about today?
- What was missing that, if put into place, would support me in being the person I have declared myself to be?
- What was missing that would have helped my self-esteem increase today?
- How will I make tomorrow better?

Chapter 23

Create a Vision for Your Life

You can't fully contribute to others until you can contribute to yourself.

If your self-image is tarnished, your expectations of participating in all the great things life has to offer are likely suffering as well. Perhaps, low self-esteem's greatest cost is the resulting resignation it fosters. We die inside a little more each day. Before we realize what is happening, we have sold out our dreams for being all we can be, having those things we deserve and living a life fueled by our passions.

We get what we expect. If we expect that our lives will be marked by rich relationships, abundance, fun and adventure, we will generate an intention to make it so. Our intention will create a drive within us to accomplish those actions necessary to manifest our vision. Likewise, if low self-esteem results in anticipation of pain, loneliness, suffering, struggle, broken relationships and poverty, we will see these results in our world. We unintentionally sabotage our efforts at achieving those things we want most because we do not believe we are worthy of receiving them. Every time things begin to look up, an invisible self-defeating inner thermostat kicks in, ensuring our low expectations become a self-fulfilling prophecy.

The good news is that you can retrain your thoughts and intentions to manifest what you want to have appear. Train your mind to become an ally in your quest for high self-esteem by creating a vision that honors your values, aligns with your passions and encompasses the qualities you are committed to fostering. This new and empowering vision will replace the current dim vision that is neither serving your magnificence nor fueling your self-esteem.

Take an 8-ounce glass filled with coffee. This represents your low self-esteem. It is murky, dark and does not transmit light. Now take a large pitcher of crystal clear water. This represents your new empowering vision. Pour the water from the pitcher into the glass. The water from the pitcher flows into the glass, causing the glass to overflow. The first few ounces have little obvious effect on the color of the liquid in the glass. However, as you add more pure water, the contents of the glass get clearer and clearer. By the time you have poured the entire pitcher into the glass, you will notice all discolored liquid is gone and only pure, clear water remains. The same holds true for your mind. As you replace cynical, self-defeating thoughts that crush your self-esteem with a positive, empowering vision that feeds your magnificence, the power of the new thoughts eventually replace the old. This elevates your esteem and dilutes the thoughts that previously consumed your attention. The power in realizing this transformation comes from the magnitude of new positive energy that far surpasses the old negative force.

To mold your new life vision, close your eyes and imagine that a genie has just appeared before you. This genie has offered to grant your every wish, provided you have the courage to envision it, believe it will happen and pursue it. In order to create this vision, you need to temporarily suspend any self-defeating thoughts that your life will bring only what you have always had. The past does not need to be a harbinger of the future. Keep in mind that we will be developing a specific plan of action to address the question, "What exactly will it take to manifest this vision?" So, create your dream vision with the expectation that we will be designing a plan to bring each aspect of it into reality.

Let's start by revisiting what values your vision will honor. These will form the fabric that will weave throughout your vision. Next, review the qualities you previously recorded that you will enhance and further develop. These qualities will speak to who you are being as you construct your ideal life. Lastly, make a list of your passions. These are those things you love to do and would gladly look forward to doing every day for the next 50 years. Your passions make life worthwhile.

Think of this vision as a movie script you will watch play out before you on the silver screen as you take your seat in the theater featuring your life story. Write your vision in first person and present tense as if you are describing a scene from the movie as it happens. Create a vivid mental image with as much detail as possible to bring your vision to life. Utilize all your senses in describing it — sight, hearing, touch, smell and taste. See your vision as an already accomplished reality in the present, not merely as something you want or hope to have happen. If you construct your vision as something you *hope* to have, you imply disappointment and the wanting, desiring and not having of it will manifest instead of the realization of the vision itself.

Include within your vision the answers to the following questions:

- Who will you be? What qualities and values will you embody? How will you look and come across to others? What will your self-image be?
- What will you do with your life when you possess these qualities and values? How will you spend a typical day at play and a typical day at work?
- What will you have as a result of embodying these qualities and behaving consistently with them? Where will you live? In what type of home and with whom? With what physical possessions will you surround yourself? What other things such as great friends, abundance, personal freedom, peace of mind, etc. will you have? What goals will you accomplish?
- Who will you assist or support with these accomplishments? Are there any special people, organizations or causes that will be an important part of your life?
- What will your relationships be like? Picture yourself interacting with friends, family, co-workers and all you meet in a way that reflects your high self-esteem and rich friendships.

You can't do this exercise wrong, so have fun creating your vision as a magnificent person worthy of the best that life has to offer.

Here is my vision, as an example:

It is September 21, 2016. My wife, Janice, and I are celebrating my 60th birthday at our winter estate in Hana, on the island of Maui, Hawaii, by hosting a party attended by a thousand of our closest friends. Our waterfront property spans several acres marked by waterfalls and lush greenery, home to hundreds of magnificent tropical birds. All our family and the close friends we've made over the past 40 years are here. Our friends look to our Hawaiian home as a place for them to relax, rest and recharge their bodies, minds and souls. Our doors are always open. We enjoy each other's company all year long during their frequent visits.

We divide our time between our winter home in Maui and our spring, summer and autumn homes in the scenic White Mountains of New Hampshire and the wonderful woods of rural Massachusetts.

Our lives have become totally devoted to contributing to others and discovering more about reaching our personal magnificence. Our company, The Center For Personal Reinvention, has guided millions of people to live rewarding lives based on choice, contribution and empowerment. People hold the center as one of the foremost organizations in the world that supports people to live lives that work optimally, in peace, harmony and happiness. We spend a large amount of time speaking, writing, coaching and inspiring others to live lives of possibility. Our goal is to kill off the resignation that consumes all too many people's lives.

My book, The Magic Lantern: A Fable About Leadership, Personal Excellence and Empowerment, *first published in 2001, just sold 20 million copies! People have found it to be a window to realize life-changing insights. The book's tale of the secrets to achieving world peace through the creation of empowering interpretations has taken hold. The thousand years of peace it foretold is well underway.*

My Power to Succeed *book series is recognized as the catalyst that has brought the personal development conversation into millions of homes. Millions have implemented its principles. It sets the new standard for creating effective communication and relationships that thrive. My book,* Restore Your Magnificence, *has supported millions of people to realize their God-given magnificence and live empowered lives, fueled by their passions and sourced by their life purposes.*

My focus, now, is on continuing personal development, both for myself and for others. I continue to champion people around the world to maximize their effectiveness, happiness and power through my public speaking engagements, transformational courses, personal coaching and writing. I am humbled by the thousands of people who have stepped forward to join us in our vision of impacting people's lives. We now work in partnership with these friends to honor our values of contribution, belonging, adventure, abundance and fun.

People the world over have learned to see networking as synonymous with contribution to others and personal growth. My story, featured on the covers of Success *and* Time *magazines, has inspired thousands to live their lives full out and with passion. We have contributed to shifting the old paradigm of struggle, suffering and resignation. Thanks to our efforts, people around the world believe in themselves and in their ability to contribute to others. Third-world countries raise billions of dollars yearly through networking enterprises patterned after my charitable programs. Due to the elevated levels of self-esteem of so many, wars are now a thing of the past. People everywhere have embraced the new paradigm of living in harmony, love, abundance and contribution to their fellow man and woman.*

We are in excellent physical health. We have abundant rich relationships. We devote time daily to our personal and spiritual development. Money is no object for us. We have all of the cars, toys and other possessions we could ever want. A large portion of the income that our organizations produce is used to fund our global humanitarian projects. We have more than enough money to support the dozens of worthwhile causes we're passionate about. Among these is quality education for all children, programs that champion the magnificence of kids all over the world and support people seeking to better themselves.

We travel the world extensively, visiting every continent and country we've ever had an interest in exploring. Many of our partners have taken on similarly rewarding lifestyles fueled by their passions. We've made friends everywhere we've traveled and have lived our lives as a daring adventure, always in search of the awesome power of possibilities.

As you can see, my vision is clear and fueled by my passions, life purpose and values. It cultivates my self-esteem through contributions to people and those ideals most important to me.

It motivates me to grow and excel, and by speaking my vision out loud, I inspire others to both join me in its realization and create empowering visions of their own.

Visions supply the creative energy that speeds the metamorphosis from caterpillar to butterfly. If we have the courage to create them, speak them aloud and believe in their ultimate realization, then visions nourish our ambitions, clarify our intentions and elevate our self-esteem. They serve as the blueprint for the magnificent castle we will build with the granite blocks of our actions and the mortar of our interpretations.

Now create your own empowering vision. Please do not pass up this opportunity to take advantage of the magic that it can unleash in transforming your life and self-image.

A vision's ultimate value is that it serves as a motivating place to come from, rather than a place to get to. Visions are also dynamic. As you achieve certain aspects of your vision, it will evolve to include new and previously unforeseen elements. Some aspects of your current vision will also change in time to no longer be part of your evolving vision, so visions always need periodic review and reevaluation. They serve to inspire and motivate you and others, not to restrict your options and vitality.

Once you have created your written vision, commit to reading it twice daily without fail, in the morning upon rising and in the evening right before bedtime. As the vision becomes an intention and expectation, your belief in its ultimate realization will support its manifestation into the world.

Thanks to Richard Brooke, author of *Mach II With Your Hair On Fire,* for his mentoring and contributions to this section on vision. This chapter is derived from his vision workshop and book.

Exercise

Write out your personal empowering vision in first person and present tense. Describe in detail what every aspect of your life will be like. Read your vision at least twice each day.

Chapter 24
Identify Your Life Purpose

Playing large and living your life purpose will handle all your fears and petty concerns.

Now that you are clear about what your most important values are and have plainly crafted a vision for your life, you are ready to focus upon clarifying your life purpose. Everyone has a life purpose. Some are living it, but most are not. If your self-esteem is low, you are not living yours fully.

Your life purpose involves finding your niche in the world's overall scheme. You are living it when your key values are honored and you spend your days alive with the vitality that results from doing what you love while sharing your gifts with the world. Your life purpose will always involve others. It will never be only self-serving or about you alone. It involves partnership and will serve your natural self-expression. Living it will feel like you are being what you were meant to be.

Your life purpose need not be complicated or lengthy to explain. In fact, it will be most powerful when spoken with a few well-chosen words. It represents the essence of who you are. Your life purpose is likely what you have been known for as far back as you can remember, especially before your self-esteem began to suffer. For many, it is what they always wanted to be or do when they were younger. Perhaps it is related to a special passion or revolves around a favorite cause or charity. It is who you authentically are at your core. When you live your life purpose, you are most alive and contributing your special gifts.

For clarity in identifying your life purpose, consider some people you most respect in the world. What specifically is it about each person that you regard highly? If you were granted one wish for the world, what would it be? If you were independently wealthy and had no restrictions placed upon you, how would you spend the rest of your life? If you could leave a legacy for the world, what would it be?

All these questions should point you in the direction of identifying those qualities or activities that would cause your life to have great meaning and your self-esteem to soar.

Here are some examples of life purposes.

- I am love.
- I show people how to laugh and have fun.
- I inspire everyone to be his or her best.
- I bring peace to the world.
- I champion women.
- I share love through pets.
- I champion equal rights.
- I inspire people to live with passion.
- I am a teacher.
- I build relationships and help people belong.
- I help people help themselves.
- I relieve suffering and help people heal.
- I advocate for the poor and helpless.
- I am a communicator.
- I champion children.
- I inspire adventure.

- I create beauty.
- I help make people's lives easier.

Special thanks go to Carol McCall. This work was adapted from her "Design Your Life Workshop."

Exercise

Consider these questions and record your answers in your journal.

- ***What is your life purpose?***
- ***How will you manifest it into the world?***
- ***What will you put into place to live it?***
- ***What key values does it honor?***
- ***How does living it elevate your self-esteem?***

Chapter 25

Set Goals and Design an Action Plan for Your Life

A vision without action is self-delusion.

Using the vision you have created, now design a plan of action that will lead toward its realization. Of course, visions are, by nature, of grand design and not typically accomplished overnight. So sort all aspects of your vision into achievable goals and actions that will support your overall objectives.

I suggest dividing your overall game plan into more specific areas to concentrate your focus:

- Health and appearance
- Wealth, finances, career, and occupation
- Relationships
- Family
- Personal and/or spiritual development
- Recreation and fun

Let's talk first about goals. Goals are objectives that you will strive to accomplish by a certain date. In other words, they are grounded in time. Powerful goals will stretch you, encourage you to grow and to risk outside your comfort zone. However, they should not be so much of a stretch that you can't realize them within your intended time frame. Goals that motivate and empower inspire action. A primary function of setting goals is to inspire you to engage in a quest for some accomplishment. The actual quest is often more important from a growth and learning perspective than the accomplishment itself. Goal-setting should serve to empower your actions and fuel your self-esteem. The label of "failure" is always an undesirable and unnecessary interpretation that we choose to skip. Instead, let's congratulate ourselves for our courage in pursuing the goals in the first place. That said, if for some reason we do not reach our goals by the expected date of accomplishment, we can simply set a new goal, knowing that we are richer because of the experience we have garnered through courageously shooting for the goal with a full effort! We simply then ask, "What was missing that might be put into place to support us to reach our next goals?"

With that said, let's get started. Examine each of the following areas in your life:

- Health and appearance
- Wealth, finances, career, and occupation
- Relationships
- Family
- Personal and/or spiritual development
- Recreation and fun

For each area, ask yourself these questions.

1. What are your long-range goals? Select a target date of five, 10 or 20 years.

2. What are your one-year goals? These can either be targets to shoot for or actions that will support your objectives.

3. What are your three-month, six-month or nine-month milestones? Milestones are interim goals you will accomplish en route to your longer-term objectives.

Some examples to the above questions follow. These examples represent the goals of a 35-year-old professional woman. Your goals will reflect your own dreams and values. The examples offered attempt to display a wide range of interests and combine both achievement and action goals.

Health and appearance

1. My five-year goal is to be my ideal weight of 125 pounds with 17 percent body fat, physically fit and healthy in mind, body and spirit. I will reflect an attractive appearance and posture as befits a person with high self-esteem. This includes having an extensive, updated wardrobe and being well-groomed with excellent dental and physical health.

2. My one-year goal is to have my dental health and appearance restored, to become physically fit through a supervised work out program and to lose 50 pounds, bringing my weight to 140 pounds.

3. My three-month milestone is to have my upper teeth capped, weigh 175 pounds and begin my training program. My six-month milestone is to weigh 155 pounds with 25

percent body fat. My nine-month milestone is to weigh 145 pounds and have 22 percent body fat.

Wealth, finances, career, occupation

1. My five-year goal is to have $100,000 in savings and work from home as the CEO of my own successful home-based business with a monthly income of $20,000. My 10-year goal is to have $250,000 in savings and to oversee an organization of 50,000 through my business, which generates a monthly income of $40,000. My 20-year goal is to be happily retired at age 55 with $5 million in my retirement account, additional assets of $10 million and a monthly residual income of $75,000.

2. My one-year goal is to pay off all my credit card debt, have $20,000 in savings and have a thriving home business that earns $6,000 per month.

3. My three-month milestone is to select a company to associate with in establishing my home-based business. My business will be firmly established, producing an income of $2,000 monthly at my six-month milestone. I will step into progressive levels of leadership and be earning $4,000 monthly at my nine-month milestone.

Relationships

1. At five years out, my relationships will be richly rewarding. I will have 100 close friends.

2. My one-year goal is to resolve all past relationships that drain my energy and detract from my happiness and self-esteem.

3. By three months, I will have contacted my friends Mark and Mary to repair our damaged relationship. I will join a social organization with the goal of making at least three new friends. At nine months, I will have joined a charitable organization and made ten new close friends.

Family

1. At five years out and beyond, my family interactions will be characterized by mutual support and loving communication. We will have a yearly family reunion to reconnect and reestablish our bonds. My relationship with my husband will be intimate and rewarding. We will have two healthy, wonderful children.

2. My one-year goal is to have clean, open and supportive communication with all my brothers and sisters. I will also have at least two "date nights" weekly with my husband.

3. At three months, I will have successfully reconnected with my estranged brother Tim. At six months, I will have hosted our first family reunion in Orlando, Florida. By nine months, I will have established weekly nurturing phone conversations with each of my brothers and sisters as well as my mom and dad. I will have set aside time every Friday and Saturday night to spend alone with my husband or with our friends.

Personal and/or spiritual development

1. At five years and beyond, I will have established myself as an accomplished listener and personal coach. I will be involved in a daily personal development program in partnership with other like-minded individuals. I will have a close relationship with God, which will be manifested by helping those less fortunate than myself. I will have co-founded a homeless shelter in Chicago, Illinois.

2. By one year out, I will have graduated from a coaching training program. I will be a member of a church that shares my views on spirituality.

3. At three months, I will have begun a year-long coaching training program. I will have established the habit of spending at least 30 minutes each day on my own personal development. This will include reading books, listening to tapes and watching videos on personal development topics. I will also have hired a personal coach to champion me with my goals and support me to remain accountable. I will have selected a church to join. I will continue with these activities throughout my first year.

Recreation and fun

1. My five-year goal is to be an intermediate-level tennis player and golfer, playing both sports at least once per week. I will also vacation at least six times yearly, traveling the world

with my husband, family and friends. My 10-year goal is to have visited every free country on the planet.

2. My one-year goal is to learn how to play tennis. I will also lower my golf handicap from 35 to 20 by playing at least twice weekly. I will have traveled to three exotic destinations with-in the next 12 months. I will spend at least one hour daily playing with my son.

3. My three-month goal will be to start my tennis and golf lessons on a weekly basis. I will have taken one vacation overseas with my spouse. I will spend at least 30 minutes each day having fun with my family. By six months, this time commitment will have increased to a minimum of one hour daily. I will have taken a second fun vacation, a Caribbean cruise with my family. By nine months, I will have taken a third vacation with my husband to Egypt.

Other Goals: BEING

1. My five-year goals include being known as a life-changing coach. I will also possess high self-esteem, which will be reflected by the qualities of humility, confidence, authenticity and care for others.

2. These same qualities will be evident one year from now.

3. These same qualities will be seen at three months and beyond. Today, I am declaring that I am a humble, confident, authentic and contributing human being.

Other Goals: DOING

1. At five years out, my work will reflect my life purpose of contributing to the poor and oppressed. This will be displayed by my public speaking in support of these causes, my work on the board of directors of the homeless shelter and through my business associations.

2. At one year, I will have become an accomplished public speaker, having spoken before an audience of at least 500 people.

3. At three months, I will have attended five Toastmasters International sessions and made three presentations to our group. At six months, I will have given my first presentation to the Chicago Pioneers women's group. At nine months, I will have spoken before a group of 100 civic leaders through my church.

Other Goals: HAVING

1. At five years out, we will own a $500,000, five-bedroom colonial home on Lake Winapog in central Michigan. I will be driving a new Jaguar convertible and my husband will have his new Jeep Cherokee.

2. My one-year goal is to move to a new home in suburban Chicago with my family.

3. My three-month milestone is to find a location in suburban Chicago to relocate my family. My six-month milestone is to

put a deposit on the land upon which we will build our home. My nine-month milestone is to begin construction on this home.

In a similar manner, write out your answers to the following questions in your journal now.

Exercise

With respect to each of the following areas:

- *Health and appearance*
- *Wealth, finances, career, and occupation*
- *Relationships*
- *Family*
- *Personal and/or spiritual development*
- *Recreation and fun*

1. *What are your long-range goals? Select either a five-year, 10-year or 20-year time frame.*

2. *What are your one-year goals?*

3. *What are your three-month, six-month or nine-month milestones?*

Chapter 26

The Power of a Daily Action Commitment

We build our self-esteem one empowering thought at a time.

There's an old riddle that asks, "How do you eat an elephant?"

The answer, of course, is, "One bite at a time!"

The concept of a daily action commitment reflects this practical wisdom. It involves a promise to take part in some definitive, specific action each and every day toward the accomplishment of your goals and in support of your new self-image. It takes advantage of the power of consistent (day-in and day-out) and persistent (until an objective is reached) activity in order to realize a worthwhile achievement. By adopting a daily action commitment in each area of your life, you will methodically make daily progress toward your goals. Your daily action commitment will need to specifically address the particular results you seek to achieve.

In the six areas of life, here are some examples of powerful daily action commitments. Each of the following is to be done on a daily basis.

Health and Appearance

- Exercise 30 minutes.
- Eat healthful, nutritious foods.
- Avoid high-fat or deep-fried foods.
- Walk 3 miles.
- Avoid alcohol and cigarettes.
- Floss your teeth.
- Brush your teeth at least three times.
- Bathe and groom.
- Dress for success whenever in public.
- Lift weights.
- Play a sport.
- Work out at a gym.

Wealth, Finances, Career, and Occupation

- Save $40 a day.
- Invest $40 a day.
- Read 30 minutes about how to manage finances.
- Send out five resumes.
- Meet two new people at work.
- Do one bold action at work that stretches you outside your comfort zone.
- Attend one course to further your education.
- Strengthen one relationship at work.

Relationships

- Make one new friend monthly.
- Connect with one old friend monthly.
- Acknowledge someone for his or her contribution to you.
- Complete a strained relationship each day until there are no strained relationships remaining.
- Champion three people in some way.

Family

- Do one nice thing for every family member.
- Tell everyone in your family that you love them.
- Forgive every family member for his or her faults.
- Tell your children something nice about them.
- Have at least one meal together as a family.
- Spend at least 30 minutes talking as a family.
- Spend at least 30 minutes of quality time with everyone in your immediate family.

Personal and/or Spiritual Development

- Read something inspirational for 30 minutes.
- Listen to personal development tapes in your car during drive time.
- Pray, meditate or worship in your own way for at least 30 minutes.
- Do something nice for someone less fortunate than you.
- Have a 30-minute coaching call.
- Participate in a 15-minute accountability report to your coaches.
- Incorporate one new personal development principle from a personal development book, such as my book, *The Power to Succeed.*

Recreation and Fun

- Spend at least 30 minutes doing something you love.
- Play a game.
- Take a walk.
- Spend 30 minutes with your fun coach. (Young children make the best fun coaches. Hire one today to be yours.)

- Do a hobby for a certain time each day.
- Do something fun with your spouse or a friend.

And, in the area of building your self-esteem,

Championing Yourself

- Acknowledge yourself for something commendable.
- Forgive someone.
- Forgive yourself.
- Treat yourself to something special.
- Develop a new habit that makes you feel good.
- Read one chapter of a personal development book.
- Listen to inspirational audio-tapes for 30 minutes.
- Have a one-hour coaching session with your coach.

Exercise

Please take a few minutes now to record your daily action commitment in each of the six areas of life.

- ***Health and appearance***
- ***Wealth, finances, career, and occupation***
- ***Relationships***
- ***Family***
- ***Personal and/or spiritual development***
- ***Recreation and fun***

Will your faithful implementation of your daily action commitment bring about the results you desire?

Daily, ask yourself, "What is missing from my daily action commitment that would better support my esteem, values, goals and vision?" Then take your answers and work them into your next day's plan.

In the same way, go through each area of your life and identify those actions that would best support your goals if performed weekly and monthly, as opposed to daily. These weekly action commitments and monthly action commitments will combine with your daily action commitments to include all regular, repeatable activities that will contribute to you being the person you have decided to be.

Dealing with Challenges

Of course, as soon as you set goals and make commitments, you can bank on challenges appearing that will threaten to derail your well-made plans. If you are pursuing your goals from the perspective of convenience instead of commitment, you will likely face a crisis when your quest is no longer very convenient. Without fear, your reasonable expectation that problems will arise, together with a firm commitment to do whatever it takes to find a way to effectively break through these challenges, will be necessary to keep yourself on the road toward your vision. Rather than fearing the onset of problems, decide to embrace them when they do show up. Every problem contains within it the gifts needed to break through. A commitment to effectively manage problems means doing whatever is necessary to stay the course. Those committed to finding a way will always find one.

Chapter 27

Put an Accountability Structure into Place

Our society firmly believes problems are bad and to be avoided and there is something wrong with people who have problems. Shift your interpretation to embrace problems and look for the gifts they conceal. Do not fall into the trap of thinking that having a problem means there is something wrong with you. Doing so will needlessly damage your self-esteem.

— Mike Smith
President, The Freedom Foundation

If you have followed along and done the exercises suggested to this point, I acknowledge you for your commitment to reinventing yourself and elevating your self-esteem. However, in spite of the best intentions, life's challenges get in the way of following through on your action plan from time to time. For this reason, your excellence will be well supported by implementing an accountability structure to ensure you follow through on what you have committed to doing.

There are many possible accountability structures you might put into place:

- Hire a coach to support your accountability and champion your progress. Many coaching organizations, including our own company, The Center for Personal Reinvention, provide expert life and business coaches to support you in deliberately designing your life and/or business.

- Get together with like-minded friends who have committed to their own life action plans. Agree to speak weekly to answer the questions we will discuss in a few moments. Call or meet with either one friend or with a small group of friends once a week.

- Create an email support group. You can create such a group for free at www.yahoogroups.com. Invite your accountability partners to report their progress either daily or weekly, depending upon what the group agrees.

These questions should take up no more than a few sentences via email. A reporting call should limit each participant to a brief five-minute report.

In your reports, briefly answer the following questions:

1. What is your daily action commitment?
2. Did you do it yesterday? If not, what did you do?
3. What worked well?
4. What was missing that, if put into place, would best support tomorrow to be better?
5. What will you do next?

Any challenges can best be addressed on a separate coaching call with the appropriate coaches present to support your progress.

It will support you to have a structure to deal with challenges as they show up. These can include:

- A mastermind group to brainstorm possibilities
- A coach to champion you and provide direction
- A resource team knowledgeable in the areas of your goals
- Research materials and references that cover the topics you seek to accomplish
- An effective time-management program that allows you to prioritize and schedule your commitments

Personal and Group Coaching Programs

The Value of Coaching to Support Your Business and Your Life

Everyone needs a coach.

In our daily lives as well as in our businesses, we typically deal with life's challenges the best we know how. If we knew what it would take to be more effective in our relationships, more productive in our activities or more successful in reaching our goals, we would surely change accordingly. The only access we ordinarily have to impact our lives comes from the areas of "what we know" and "what we don't know." In our efforts to achieve more, we usually resort to increasing what we do know by learning to do things a little better, a little differently or we simply do more of a behavior that produced a certain result for us in the past. This behavior can produce small, incremental increases in our ability to impact our business and our world. Likewise, by educating ourselves in the arena of "what we don't know," this knowledge then becomes part of what we now do know: If you are computer illiterate and you learn how to adeptly operate a computer, you will have successfully converted something that you do not know into what you now know. More than 95 percent of our efforts are spent in these two arenas – what we know and what we don't know.

However, our most extraordinary growth comes from outside the arena of what we know or don't know. This composes the vast variety of ideas that we are blind to, not knowing that they even exist. It's in this arena of "what we don't know we don't know" that breakthroughs occur.

So how do you gain access to this fertile territory if you don't even know that it exists? The answer lies in recruiting the help of a coach who can support you to explore this rich domain that is outside of your customary perspective and behaviors. Your coaches should be individuals who possess the key principles that make them powerful in the particular arena they offer coaching.

A coach may be powerful in some arenas but not necessarily in others. The same person who is qualified to coach you in business matters may be totally unqualified to coach you in the area of relationships or spiritual matters. True coaches do not give advice or lend their opinions. They are value based, not ego based. They do not manipulate or exploit to carry out their own agenda. They are totally nonjudgmental. They are not the same as counselors or therapists. They do not try to protect, control or rescue those they are coaching.

They instead listen for where you may be experiencing challenges or may be missing some key element that, if put into place, would produce a desired change. Coaches support us in seeing something that we may not be aware of by listening both to what we say and to what we leave out. They empathize with the person being coached, but they are not emotionally attached to an outcome. They serve to champion people to have their lives work optimally. They do this by asking questions, exploring possibilities, making requests and, at times, confronting issues that may need to be examined. Skilled coaching is a fine art and a highly valuable service.

For a coaching relationship to be possible, there must exist an open willingness on the part of the person being coached to endure and actively participate in the process. Of course, total confidentiality must exist to allow for the freedom to explore any and all areas necessary. The absence of judging and advice creates the opening needed to fully examine any possibility.

Coaching is typically undertaken in any of six major areas of life: business/career, health, wealth, relationships, spirituality/personal development or recreation/passions. A good coach will clarify if his or her coaching client is open to explore any or all of these areas or if the coaching relationship is agreed to be limited to any one or more areas. True coaches interact with honor and respect while, at the same time, they are not reluctant to call someone on their "stuff" out of a solid commitment to champion the person's excellence and best interests.

Successful coaches:

- Listen for what may be missing to accomplish a result or honor a person's values.
- Lead by example and champion others to step into leadership.
- Commit themselves to pursuing their client's excellence and, yet, are not attached to his or her responses.
- Ground themselves in value-based personal development principles.
- Hold those they coach as totally capable and competent while looking for what might be missing for them to fully experience their magnificence.
- Nurture the client to be their best and live with passion while accomplishing their goals.
- Never make the client feel small or dependent.
- Champion the client to be the best they can be while staying "invisible" as a coach. The coach's ego must not be a factor in the relationship.
- Tell the truth and do not step over uncomfortable topics or situations in order to avoid discomfort or look good.
- Create a safe atmosphere that allows the client to be vulnerable and open to possibilities.
- Support their coaching clients in an accountability structure, ensuring that they follow through on what they say they will do.

- Support the free flow of ideas and conversations for possibilities through idea streaming.

It is helpful for any coaching relationship to begin by developing clarity with respect to the client's overall vision. This vision should include every aspect of the person's life and business. From this wide-ranging perspective, it is then possible to develop a plan to accomplish any goals. These goals blend into the big picture by fulfilling or working toward one aspect of the vision's realization.

A productive coaching relationship can focus on either a life or business project. In the realm of business, a coaching relationship is often best undertaken within the context of a project or action plan that is grounded in time. By focusing on producing specific and measurable results, a coach can support a client to best work through any business obstacles or life challenges en route to the accomplishment of one's goals. A coach can also assist in gaining clarity on all conditions of satisfaction that may be important to a project's fulfillment. Such conditions might include those non-measurable items that would need to take place for a project to be considered a success: developing stronger relationships with family members, spending quality time with children, devoting a minimum amount of time daily to meeting one's own needs, taking a well deserved vacation, etc.

Many people mistakenly assume that they can be successful in business without being successful in other areas of their lives. While important, our businesses form only one component of our lives. If there is an imbalance in any of the six prominent areas of our lives, any business accomplishment will somehow fall incomplete. For this reason, a good coach will support a client to adopt a whole-thinking perspective with mastery of all areas of life as the ultimate goal. For this reason, personal development is an essential component of any business coaching relationship. As one undertakes the personal improvement process, increased business productivity will surely result.

Just as an Olympic athlete in pursuit of a gold medal would not think of undertaking such an accomplishment without the support of a coach, most people would also benefit from a coaching relationship. Coaching can add fun and excitement to every aspect of your life as you take on the challenge of reinventing yourself and your business, always in search of excellence. And of course, one of the major benefits of an ongoing coaching relationship is that you will develop the coaching skills yourself that will be necessary for you to impact the lives of others. If you are in business and do not yet have a coach who is committed to championing your success, I strongly encourage you to look into how such a relationship might support your goals and move your business and life forward with velocity.

Hire a Coach

The Center for Personal Reinvention offers individual and group coaching programs that support people to realize their business and life goals while designing a life of choice and without regrets. For more information on hiring a coach, please contact me at DrJRubino@email.com or by calling (888) 821-3135.

Chapter 28

Acknowledge Yourself Daily

All the extraordinary men I have known were extraordinary in their own estimation.
— President Woodrow T. Wilson

By now, you can see how taking responsibility for living in alignment with your vision can give you fulfillment and passion while honoring your values. This, in turn, can only help raise your self-esteem. Still, if you are accustomed to judging yourself harshly, you will need to recognize this tendency and decide instead to acknowledge yourself for some worthy accomplishment on a daily basis.

Get into the habit of noticing those things you do well. Acknowledge yourself with praise every time you catch yourself doing something commendable. As you better recognize numerous occasions to excel, you will champion yourself to reach new heights on a regular basis.

As you go about your day, visualize opportunities to be proud of yourself as if you are standing at a fork in the road. To the left of the fork lies the possibility of acting as you often have, in a way that lowers your self-opinion. This path involves blame, fault and "shoulds." It means taking the easy, familiar way out, only to regret your decision later. It may look like doing what is convenient, hiding from your power, not communicating forcefully or fearfully selling out the other person by stepping over something. It may mean choosing to look good or be liked instead of following your intuition or conscience.

The other pathway, the path of the heart, involves risking courageously as you honor your values. It means telling the truth and acting in sync with your commitments. It is doing what you know in your heart is the right thing. When you decide to take this path, you build self-esteem by living in harmony with your vision.

The more you decide to consciously take this path, the easier the choice becomes. So, to build your self-esteem, become proficient at championing yourself and acknowledge your achievements each time for a job well done.

Always remember, as human beings, we are not perfect. Whenever you err, simply forgive yourself, clean up any damage and recommit to do better next time. It is by forgiving and loving yourself first that you will then be able to forgive and love others. By building your own self-esteem, you will have the ability to champion others to do likewise.

Select one or more acknowledgment partners and agree to support each other daily with the following exercise.

Exercise

Each day, identify something special about you. Catch yourself doing something commendable. Look for a value that distinguishes you as a worthy, even extraordinary, human being. Select a quality that describes you or your progress in your personal development plan. Recognize a special strength you see in yourself. Then write at least a 100-word paragraph describing how you embody this characteristic. Write your paragraph as though you are honoring a very dear and special friend at an awards banquet. Modesty has no place in this exercise. Your report must be a proud and expressive acknowl-

edgment of your magnificence with regard to this point.

Have your acknowledgment partners do the same regarding an admirable quality for which they will each recognize themselves. If you are all on email, send your summary to each other daily in that way. If not, fax, mail or read your acknowledgments to each other each day without fail.

Rate your partner's paragraph on a 1 to 10 scale, with 10 being a great job in acknowledging his special attribute. If you rate your partner's performance as less than 10, suggest what you see missing to have him realize his greatness with respect to the trait being acknowledged.

Here are three examples of acknowledging such a tribute.

Trait: *Courage*

Today I acknowledge myself for my awesome courage. I am a brave and extraordinary human being. I could have very easily wallowed in the self-pity that would kill my spirit and have me forego my dreams and hide out, but that is not who I am. I got dressed this morning and went to the gym with the goal of making at least one new friend. With this commitment in mind, I sought out several people to say hello to and exchanged smiles and pleasantries. I selected a treadmill next to the person I targeted to be my friend. I smiled, complimented her on her dedication to her workout and introduced myself. She did likewise, and before we knew it, we realized we had quite a bit in common. The time passed quickly as we learned more about each other. I discovered that we both enjoy playing tennis. I asked her if she might like to play sometime, and she was thrilled at the suggestion. She also suggested that we make plans to work out together again. I am so proud of myself for displaying such incredible courage and determination. I am a very courageous lady and I made a great friend!

Trait: *Great Listener*

Today I acknowledge myself as a great listener. This quality is a tremendous contribution to other people. Rather than focus upon my own agenda, I often offer the gift of listening to heal others. I listen without judgment and without interrupting. People who speak to me really come away from the conversation with a sense of being heard. This is a tremendous way to support others to work through their problems as I validate their own self-worth. As I continue to listen to others, I am offering this great gift of mine. Each time I contribute to raising someone's self-image by allowing them to be heard, I do the same for myself. What an awesome and valuable person I am!

Trait: *Forgiveness*

Today I acknowledge myself for forgiving. I have given up my right to pity myself and recognize that everyone makes mistakes. The first person I forgave today is myself. I realize all I can do every day is do the best I can. When I mess up, all I need do is recognize my mistake, forgive myself and commit to doing better next time. I also forgive my husband, Bill, for losing his temper with me. I know that he is doing the best he knows how. When he yells at me, it's about him, and I refuse to take it personally. I forgive him for these lapses and show him love in return each time. I see this does wonders in having him calm down and realize his lack of patience. I see how this quality is a tremendous support to my happiness. What a great human being I am!

Exercise

Commit to doing this action daily for at least the next 30 days. It will soon become a habit that will support you in recognizing all your outstanding qualities.

Chapter 29

Take Responsibility for Your Needs by Making Requests

Ask and you shall receive. Seek and you shall find. Knock and the door will be opened.
— Matthew 7:8

As human beings, we all possess a variety of needs that must be met for us to lead fulfilled and happy lives. These needs range from basic physical needs like proper nutrition, clothing and shelter to equally important emotional needs such as the need to love and be shown love, the need to belong and the need to be respected. We also need physical intimacy on both a sexual and emotional level. As these needs are met, other needs appear. These include intellectual needs such as the need to pursue fulfilling work, the need to play and have fun recreationally and the need to seek meaning in life. Those lacking in self-esteem often forego their needs, resigned to not having them fulfilled because they're not worthy.

A habit that will support maintaining high self-esteem is to assume total responsibility for making life work optimally. This translates into seeing to it that all your needs are met. Responsibility is never about blame, burden or fault. It doesn't involve judgment, guilt or shame. It lives only in the present as a form of empowerment, never in the past as a way to reinforce a negative past opinion. All too often, our society holds responsibility as a concept that limits, binds and makes us wrong. We see responsibility as something to avoid rather than something that serves our excellence.

In contrast to this definition, I invite you to consider responsibility as a gift that can support your life to work most favorably. Think about responsibility from the perspective that it is your right to actively meet your needs, nurture your grandeur and bring about your happiness. Take the interpretation it is your obligation to ensure that all aspects of your life contribute to your enrichment and happiness. From this perspective, you are the source of everything that appears in your world. If your intention is to live well and with high self-esteem, you will need to bring these conditions to bear by living intentionally. You are worthy of the best life has to offer. To justify logic that keeps your needs from being met needlessly detracts from the quality of your life and reinforces low self-esteem.

Life is a dance and it takes at least two people to participate. If you do not like the dance step you're doing, it's up to you to change your step. When you do so, others will follow and change their step as well. You must train others how they are to interact with you. If you find that people are not honoring your values or showing you sufficient respect, take responsibility for shifting your part in the dance. Refuse to put up with abusive or condescending behavior that is not appropriate for the person you have decided to be.

One way you can accomplish the intention to honor your needs is by making powerful requests. Too often, those lacking self-esteem fail to ask for what they want or need. This stems from the feeling of being unworthy of receiving. Those with low self-esteem often focus on meeting other people's needs in place of their own. They often refrain from asking for what they want due to a fear of being rejected. They rely on the distorted logic that they can't be turned down if they don't ask. What they fail to realize is that they also won't get what they want if they don't have the courage to identify what that is and ask for it.

Requests are the engines that move the action train forward. Daily, pay attention to how you can impact situations and get people moving in a positive direction by making requests of them. To powerfully make your requests, direct them to the specific people who are best able to act upon the requests. Make your request's meaning clear and grounded in time with a specific date by which to honor it. A powerful request might be phrased, "I request that you take *x* action, by *y* date." Also take into consideration what you know about the other person to appreciate why he or she should honor the request.

By creating an understanding for the reasons behind the request and any details that support its being granted, you stand a much greater chance of the other person comprehending, appreciating and honoring it. Your request more likely will be honored when it is simple, direct, easily understood and can be readily met. Keep your request clean of blame or insinuations that makes someone else wrong. Speak your request powerfully as would a person with high self-esteem. Your confident posture and the nonjudgmental positive energy you communicate will support you in being heard and having your request honored.

By making clear, specific requests directly of those who can honor your needs, you take responsibility for ensuring your life works optimally. Remember that with all requests, the other person has the option to comply with the request, decline it, make a counteroffer or ask for more time to consider the request. Your power results from making requests with an expectation they be honored but without an attachment to it. For the other person to not be coerced into complying with your request, she must have the space to decline it if it does not work for her.

Remember, whether someone accepts or declines your request has nothing to do with your value as a person. When you make requests, your ability to give other people valid reasons to seriously consider your request will support your success. Whenever possible, show how meeting your request will mutually benefit them. Your asking for it will elevate your self-esteem. Realize your ability to impact your world with confidence and velocity.

Exercise

Daily, make at least three requests that honor your value as a worthy person.

Chapter 30

Champion Others to Have High Self-Esteem

The quality of our lives is directly proportional to the quality of our relationships. In order to make relationships work, we must give others the space to be any way they are, without judgment. When it is all right with you for them to be who they are, you create room for them to be. They will show up in that space and the relationship will work.

— Dr. Tom Ventullo
President, The Center for Personal Reinvention

The secret to championing others to have high self-esteem is to create room for their humanity. Applying this same wisdom to yourself will elevate your own self-esteem. By suspending judgment on a moment-by-moment basis and giving up your right to excessively control or dominate others, you allow them the privilege to be who they are without an attachment to changing them. There is a big difference between being committed to someone's excellence and being emotionally invested in the outcome you expect. Look for and use every opportunity to acknowledge others for their positive qualities and the glimpses of emerging qualities you would like to see more of in them. Believing in others' magnificence, even before they believe it themselves, champions them to step into these possibilities. This is true for both children and adults. When we can allow people the freedom to be whoever they are by making room for their humanity, we create an opening for them to grant us that same luxury. This creates an energy that supports open communication and availability to change.

The same applies to us. When we learn to suspend self-judgment and have compassion for our own humanity, we give up our right to beat ourselves up over and over for not living up to our unrealistic expectations. We create room for ourselves to make mistakes by forgiving ourselves as often as necessary while committing to learning and doing better next time. We appreciate and praise those qualities in ourselves that work well while seeking to improve those that do not contribute to our excellence. This understanding attitude and self-love creates space for us to learn and grow, just as it does for others.

What we resist, we keep in place. This is the nature of wars, upsets and suffering. We can always find plenty of reasons to judge others (and ourselves) harshly. Judging others critically makes us right and them wrong. It allows us to dominate them and avoid being dominated. It gives us a temporary feeling of superiority that fades away into the regret of broken relationships and strife.

The antidote to the unending cycle of judgment, domination, suffering and low self-esteem is love. When we love and forgive ourselves, we give ourselves permission to be human, permission to make mistakes and mess things up. This, in turn, allows us to forgive and offer love to others. We go from being attached to the need that others meet our high expectations to being committed to their excellence instead. Giving up this same attachment to perfection in favor of a commitment to excellence supports us as well. When we act this way with our children, we find that responding always with love and without judgment supports their thriving self-esteem, allowing them to pursue excellence rather than perfection. While we certainly do not condone hurtful or inappropriate behavior, seeing such actions as resulting from an unmet need gives us better insight on how to best support this person's growth. Always remember, we are not our behaviors. Unworkable behaviors can be changed. It is critical that we not judge others or ourselves as intrinsically bad or worthless simply because our behavior is unacceptable.

In the beginning of this book, we discussed the power of creating empowering interpretations that allow for empathy and forgiveness and that support relationships to flourish. This is the power of love. In times of stress and upset, ask yourself the questions:

- What would I do now if my actions were based in love?
- What would I do if I really loved myself?
- How would I respond if I truly loved the other person?

Doing so will give you the power to forgive, the power to create and the power to restore your own magnificence as you support magnificence in others.

Lastly, realize we all have lived with the false hope that life will be great somewhere down the road, but only when some particular event happens: maybe leaving home, moving to another state, getting married, having children or getting divorced.

Why put it off as if happiness can only happen in the future? Life can be great today, and the power to make it fulfilling and magnificent already lies with you, not with that event. Decide today to be happy. Know that you are a glorious being who, by being born, has taken on an exceedingly challenging struggle. Fall in love with the magnificent person you are. Realize no one else on the planet possesses your unique combination of qualities, gifts and talents. Acknowledge yourself for these often.

Forgive yourself for having fallen short of perfection and offer this same forgiveness to those who have erred, hurting you in the process. Grant yourself the understanding, respect and compassion that you would gladly give your dearest, most trusted friend. Know that you need not continue to judge yourself so harshly.

Embracing acceptance succeeds when you recognize, moment by moment, when you are judging yourself and immediately return to your commitment to love yourself and look for your splendor instead of your shortcomings. Expect a better future and commit to the actions necessary to realize your vision. Live boldly and with passion, and watch your self-esteem and that of others flourish.

A Final Note

Reclaiming self-esteem can take some time to accomplish. After all, it has taken many years for your negative self-talk to take its toll. The direction this book provides will be sufficient for many to move their lives toward a positive track to restore significant self-belief.

For others, they'll need the support of a psychotherapist or coach trained in championing people to restore their self-esteem. Do not hesitate to seek support in restoring your self-image. Ask your physician or local hospital for some suggestions to locate a professional skilled in this area. Self-esteem therapy has proven to successfully help people regain their sense of worth. It's important to remember that help is always available and it is your responsibility to yourself to do whatever it takes to feel good about who you are so you can live a happy, fulfilling life.

12 Steps to Restoring Your Self-Esteem

1. Identify the source of your low self-esteem.
   What negative thoughts did you buy into or interpret about yourself? What new positive interpretations can you create?
2. Construct a list of your negative qualities and one describing your strengths. Develop a plan to work on the qualities you wish to manifest.
3. Identify lingering upsets from your past. Take action to complete each one and move on with your life in a positive, productive manner.
4. Decide today to forgive those who have hurt you as you likewise forgive yourself. Design an action plan to address and complete each strained relationship.
5. Design a specific dated plan to remove yourself from any abusive relationships. Inform people in your life of your commitment to reinvent yourself and notify them that you will no longer permit others to treat you without respect.
6. Practice creating new empowering interpretations daily about yourself.
7. Create a detailed newly invented declaration about who you are that addresses every aspect of your self-image.
8. Visualize your new positive self and create a vivid movie script of what your future will look like. Read your vision at least twice daily, upon rising and before bed.
9. Create a series of positive affirmations based upon your vision. Write these on index cards and position them where you will see them throughout your day. Create an audiotape of your new affirmations and listen to the tape at least twice daily.
10. Surround yourself with people and things that reflect your self-respect and honor your worth as a person.
11. Every night before bedtime, acknowledge yourself for some worthy accomplishment achieved that day.
12. Create an accountability support group to report your weekly progress in honoring yourself and meeting your goals. Seek professional assistance if needed.

Dr. Joe Rubino is widely acknowledged as one of North America's foremost success and productivity coaches. He is the CEO of Visionary International Partnerships. To date, more than 500,000 people have benefited from his writing, coaching and leadership development training. Together with Dr. Tom Ventullo, he is the co-founder of The Center For Personal Reinvention, an organization that provides coaching and productivity and leadership development courses that champion people to maximize their personal power and effectiveness.

Also by Dr. Joe Rubino:

- *The Power to Succeed: 30 Principles for Maximizing Your Personal Effectiveness*
- *The Power to Succeed: More Principles for Powerful Living, Book II*
- *The Magic Lantern: A Fable About Leadership, Personal Excellence and Empowerment*
- *Secrets of Building a Million-Dollar Network-Marketing Organization from a Guy Who's Been There, Done That and Shows You How to Do It Too*
- *10 Weeks to Network Marketing Success: The Secrets to Launching Your Very Own Million-Dollar Organization* in a 10-week business-building and personal-development self-study course (6 audio cassettes and workbook)

To request information about any of The Center For Personal Reinvention's programs or to order any of Dr. Rubino's books, visit www.CenterForPersonalReinvention.com

Recommended Personal Development Programs

The Center For Personal Reinvention

Dr. Joe Rubino and Dr. Tom Ventullo

Where are you blocked in your life and in your business?
Where is there an unacceptable level of resignation or conflict?
Where are there interpersonal listening and communication skills lacking?
Where are you lacking partnership, commitment and vision?

The world we live and work in is marked by unprecedented change and fraught with new and complex challenges. For many of us, life begins to look like an uphill struggle to survive instead of a fun and exciting opportunity to grow, risk and live your dreams in partnership with others. The stresses, conflicts and frustrations we experience daily need not be so.

There exists another possibility.

... To live and work with passion —
empowered by the challenges of life.

... To champion others to achieve excellence in a nurturing environment that fosters partnerships.

... To acquire the success principles that support mutuality, creativity and harmony.

... To take on the art of listening and communicating in such a way that others are impacted to see new possibilities for accomplishment, partnership and excellence.

Reinventing ourselves, our relationships and our perception of the world is the result of a never-ending commitment to our own personal magnificence and to that of others. It is made possible through acquiring approximately 50 key principles that cause people to begin to view life and people in an entirely different way. When people really get these principles, life, relationships, and new possibilities for breakthroughs show up from a totally fresh perspective. Through the use of cutting-edge technology as a vibrant basis for learning, growing and acting, The Center For Personal Reinvention successfully supports people to view life with a new and fresh awareness as they self-discover these life-changing principles.

With this program, YOU will:

- Uncover the secrets to accessing your personal power while maximizing your productivity.
- Gain clarity on exactly what it will take to reach your goals with velocity.
- Create a structure for skyrocketing your effectiveness while developing new and empowering partnerships.
- Learn how taking total responsibility for every aspect of your life and business can result in breakthrough performance.
- Discover the key elements of a detailed action plan and how to reach your goals in record time.
- Acquire the keys to listening and communicating effectively and intentionally.
- Recognize and shift out of self-defeating thoughts and actions.

- Gain the insight to better understand others with new compassion and clarity.
- Learn how to develop the charisma necessary to attract others to you.
- Experience the confidence and inner peace that comes from stepping into leadership.

The Center for Personal Reinvention

...Transferring the Power to Succeed!

Customized Courses and Programs Personally Designed
For Achieving Maximum Results

Areas of Focus Include:

Designing Your Future
Making Life and Businesses Work
Generating Infinite Possibilities
Creating Conversations for Mutuality
Commitment Management
Personal Coaching and Development
Maximizing Personal Effectiveness
Breakthrough Productivity
Leadership Development
Relationship and Team Building
Conflict Resolution
Listening for Solutions
Systems for Personal Empowerment
Personal and Productivity Transformation

Designing Structures for Accomplishment
Creating Empowered Listening Styles
Possibility Thinking
Forwarding Action
Structures for Team Accountability
Innovative Thinking
Completing with the Past
Creating a Life of No Regrets

The Center For Personal Reinvention champions companies and individuals to achieve their potential through customized programs addressing specific needs consistent with their vision for the future.

Contact us today to explore how we might impact your world!

The Center For Personal Reinvention
PO Box 217
Boxford, MA 01921
drjrubino@email.com
Tel: (888) 821-3135
Fax: (630) 982-2134

Other Personal Development Books by Dr. Joe Rubino

The Power to Succeed: 30 Principles for Maximizing Your Personal Effectiveness

What exactly distinguishes those who are effective in their relationships, productive in business and happy, powerful and successful in their approach to life from those who struggle, suffer and fail? That is the key question that *The Power to Succeed: 30 Principles for Maximizing Your Personal Effectiveness*, supports readers to explore in life-changing detail. The information, examples, experiences and detailed exercises offered will produce life-altering insights for readers who examine who they are being on a moment to moment basis that either contributes to increasing their personal effectiveness, happiness and power — or not. As you commit to exploring what it takes to reach your personal power, you will gain the tools to overcome any challenges or limiting thoughts and behavior. Discover exactly what it means to be the best you can be.

With this book YOU will:

- Uncover the secrets to accessing your personal power.
- Create a structure for maximizing your effectiveness with others.
- Learn to take total responsibility for everything in your life.
- Discover the key elements to accomplishment and how to reach your goals in record time.

- Identify your life rules and discover how honoring your core values can help you maximize productivity.
- Resolve issues from your past and design your future with deliberate intent.
- Discover the keys to communicating effectively and intentionally.
- Stop complaining and start doing.
- Seize your personal power and conquer resignation in your life.
- Learn how to generate conversations that uncover new possibilities.
- See how embracing problems can lead to positive breakthroughs in life.
- Leave others whole while still realizing the power of telling the truth.
- Learn how to develop the charisma necessary to attract others to you.

The Power to Succeed: More Principles for Powerful Living, Book II

This revealing book continues where *The Power to Succeed: 30 Principles for Maximizing Your Personal Effectiveness* left off with more powerful insights into what it takes to be most happy, successful and effective with others.

With this book YOU will:

- Discover the keys to unlock the door to success and happiness.

- Learn how your listening attitude determines what you attract to you.
- Learn to shift your listening attitude to access your personal power.
- See how creating a clear intention can cause miracles to show up around you.
- Learn the secrets to making powerful requests to get what you want from others.
- Discover how to fully connect with and champion others to realize their greatness.
- Learn to create interpretations that support your excellence and avoid those that keep you small.
- Develop the power to speak and act from your commitments.
- See how communication with others can eliminate unwanted conditions from your life.
- Discover the secret to being happy and eliminating daily upsets.
- Learn how to put an end to gossip and stop giving away your power.
- Develop the ability to lead your life with direction and purpose and discover what it's costing you not to do so.
- And more!!

The Power to Succeed: 30 Principles for Maximizing Your Personal Effectiveness and its sequel, *The Power to Succeed: More Principles for Powerful Living, Book II*, are a powerful course in becoming the person you wish to be. Read these books, take on the success principles discussed and watch your life and business transform and flourish.

The Magic Lantern: A Fable About Leadership, Personal Excellence and Empowerment

Set in the magical world of Center Earth, inhabited by dwarves, elves, goblins and wizards, *The Magic Lantern* is a tale of personal development that teaches the keys to success and happiness. This fable examines what it means to take on true leadership while learning to become maximally effective with everyone we meet.

A renowned personal development trainer, coach and veteran author, Dr. Joe Rubino tells the story of a group of dwarves and their young leader who go off in search of the secrets to a life that works, a life filled with harmony and endless possibilities and void of the regrets and upsets that characterize most people's existence. With a mission to restore peace and harmony to their village in turmoil, the little band overcomes the many challenges they face along their eventful journey. Through self-discovery, they develop the principles necessary to be the best that they can be as they step into leadership and lives of contribution to others.

The Magic Lantern teaches us such noble lessons as:

- the power of forgiveness
- the meaning of responsibility and commitment
- what leadership is really all about
- the magic of belief and positive expectation
- the value of listening as an art
- the secret to mastering one's emotions and actions
- and much more.

It combines the spellbinding story telling reminiscent of Tolkien's *The Hobbit* with the personal development tools of the great masters.

ORDER COUPON

Yes, I want to invest in my future!
Please send me the following books by Dr. Joe Rubino.

Book Title	Price	Qty.
The Power to Succeed: 30 Principles for Maximizing Your Personal Effectiveness	$15.95	
The Power to Succeed: More Principles for Powerful Living, Book II	$15.95	
The Magic Lantern: A Fable About Leadership, Personal Excellence and Empowerment	$15.95	
Subtotal		
MA residents add 5% sales tax		
Shipping and Handling ($4.95 for the first book plus $2 each additional book; $9.95 per book for non-US/Canadian orders)		
Total		

Name ______________________________

Address ______________________ City ______________ State _____

Zip ___________ Email_______________ Tel: ______________

I'd like to pay by:

☐ Credit Card Circle one: MasterCard VISA American Express

Credit Card Number ______________________________

Expiration Date __________ Signature ______________________

☐ Check or Money Order Enclosed (US Funds Only)

☐ I am interested in learning more about The Center For Personal Reinvention's programs including coaching services.

Please place this order form with payment into an envelope and mail to:
Vision Works Publishing
PO Box 217
Boxford, MA 01921

Or To Order:
Call (888) 821-3135 Fax: (630) 982-2134
Email: VisionWorksBooks@Email.com

QUANTITY DISCOUNTS AVAILABLE

Index

Topics

Topics

T o p i c s

Topics